Between the

Dragon
and the
Eagle

Between the
Dragon
and the
Eagle

Mical Schneider

 HOUGHTON MIFFLIN BOSTON • MORRIS PLAINS, NJ

California • Colorado • Georgia • Illinois • New Jersey • Texas

For Michael

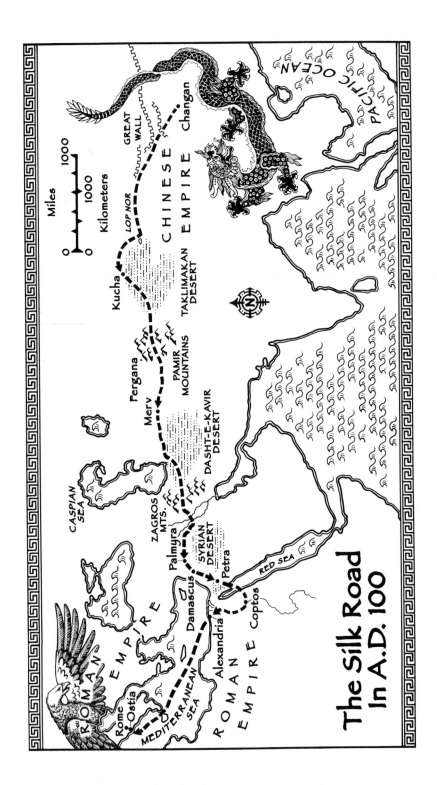

The Silk Road
In A.D. 100

PACIFIC OCEAN

CHINESE EMPIRE

GREAT WALL

Changan

LOP NOR

Kucha

TAKLIMAKAN DESERT

Fergana

PAMIR MOUNTAINS

Merv

DASHT-E-KAVIR DESERT

CASPIAN SEA

ZAGROS MTS.

Palmyra

SYRIAN DESERT

Petra

RED SEA

Damascus

Alexandria

Coptos

ROMAN EMPIRE

Rome

Ostia

MEDITERRANEAN SEA

ROMAN EMPIRE

Miles

1000

1000

Kilometers

N

Preface

Two thousand years ago, China made the twisting, fire-breathing dragon the symbol of its power and good fortune. Half a world away, Rome adopted the proud eagle as the image of its own nobility and strength. The two empires were the strongest powers on earth. China dominated the Asian continent, and Rome controlled most of Europe and the Middle East. The skillful rulers of these two empires built cities, encouraged the arts, and supported complex technology.

At the time of this story, the year A.D. 100, the emperor Trajan governed in Rome. The Chinese, who called themselves the Han people, lived under the rule of the emperor Han Ho Ti. Both emperors used armies to keep order, to amass great wealth, and to spread

their respective language and culture far beyond their borders. Roman and Chinese governments thrived under the supervision of able nobles and educated commoners. Within the cities, merchants developed flourishing markets, or bazaars, and extended the scope of their trading to bring in new goods from distant lands. In the countryside, farmers either worked on large estates owned by nobles or cultivated small fields beside their villages. Beggars, criminals, and slaves existed in both empires. Despite their similarities, however, the rulers and peoples of Rome and China never met.

The two empires were separated by thousands of miles of harsh terrain. On one side of each empire was an ocean. The Atlantic lay west of Rome, and the Pacific was east of China. Deserts spread in endless waves between these two great powers. The formidable Taklimakan Desert covered most of western China. A series of equally dangerous deserts—the Dasht-e-Kavir in Iran, the Syrian Desert east of the city of Damascus, and the Negev Desert in Israel—stretched eastward from the edge of the Roman Empire. Almost halfway along the route from China to Rome (near the modern borders of Russia, Afghanistan, and China) rose the perpetually snowcapped and glacial Pamir Mountains. Broad rivers, subject to uncontrollable spring floods, lapped against wide floodplains. These plains offered flat fertile fields for farming but held the threat of

insect-borne diseases. Unbearable heat, winter bliz-
zards, and monsoon rains beset the two empires.
Crossing from one to the other was generally considered not only dangerous but nearly impossible.

Yet a handful of merchants dared to make the trip.
In the first century A.D., small bands of travelers—usu-
ally made up of men and boys—set out in a series of
long, dusty caravans. They followed worn camel paths
that linked oases (natural desert springs), market towns,
and regional highways. The routes were identified by
word of mouth and by an occasional simple map.

At market towns and on the road, the traders stayed
at caravansaries, inns built to accommodate hundreds
of people and camels. The travelers sold their original
wares at bustling markets and bought new goods. In
the towns, the traders learned foreign languages. They
encountered different religions—Christianity, Judaism,
and pagan beliefs in the Roman Empire, and Bud-
dhism, Taoism, and Confucianism in the Chinese Empire. Often travelers carried these new ideas with them
to the next marketplace.

The merchants' route is called the Silk Road because
silk was the one item that made the complete journey
from China to Rome. Silk came in many shades and
textures. Some bolts were as vivid and light as a but-
terfly's wing, while others were stiff and heavy.
Wealthy Romans—especially those who had the distinc-
tion of being Roman citizens—willingly paid high prices

for silk. They valued it because it was supple, strong, and beautiful and also because it was rare and difficult to acquire. Wearing silk became a mark of status and prestige in Roman society.

How did the Silk Road work? In A.D. 100, a merchant in China wishing to sell silk would organize a caravan. He would either head the expedition himself or hire a trader to take the merchandise westward. At the Great Wall, the trader left China proper and entered the Western Regions, an area inhabited by wandering herders. Many Chinese considered the nomads of the Western Regions to be barbarians because they did not farm or follow Chinese ways. The common people looked down upon merchants and traders who came in contact with these nomads. Once past the desert, which is part of present-day Xinjiang Province in China, the trader crossed the Pamir Mountains to the Parthian city of Merv in modern Turkmenistan.

At Merv the Chinese merchant sold his silk to a Parthian trader who took the fabric to Palmyra, an ancient city whose ruins are in modern Syria. The silk was sold again in Palmyra, and a new merchant carried it from Palmyra to Petra, in modern Jordan. The last trader transported it from Petra to Alexandria, Egypt, and then to Rome, Italy. Hand over hand, from one merchant to another, the silk slowly crossed deserts, mountains, and rivers. The silk, not the trader, made the journey from China to Rome.

Every successful stage of the trip was the result of courage, hard work, and a measure of good luck. Merchants faced relentless deserts, vicious robbers, mountain avalanches, blinding sandstorms, and dry oases. In general they traveled with only their wits and simple weapons. As trade increased, governments provided troops to patrol the roads and workers to repair them. Over time the merchants in the bazaars developed standard weights for goods and coinage. Travel became safer and more routine.

Two thousand years ago, the Silk Road brought together, in peace, trust, and prosperity, the people of the ancient world. This fictional story of one journey on the Silk Road represents the experiences of many of its unknown—but quite real—travelers and traders.

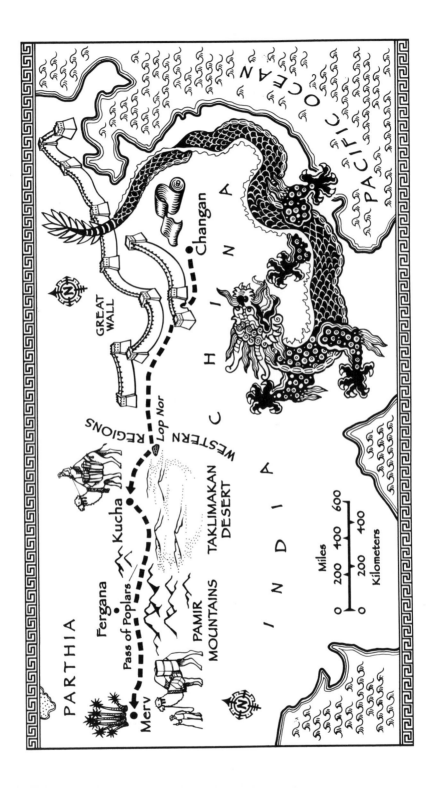

PACIFIC OCEAN

GREAT WALL

Changan

C H I N A

WESTERN REGIONS

Lop Nor

TAKLIMAKAN DESERT

PAMIR MOUNTAINS

Kucha

Pass of Poplars

Fergana

PARTHIA

Merv

INDIA

Miles
0   200   400   600

Kilometers
0   200   400

The Blue Silk
Travels from
Changan to Merv

Chapter 1

$\mathbf{H}$an Tzu paused before the elegant shop in Changan, the great trading city of central China. In the gray dawn, a few flakes of late winter snow drifted past his smooth, round face and onto his sheepskin cloak. He barely noticed. Instead he concentrated on his meeting with Yin Li. With a single word, this wealthy merchant could grant Han Tzu's most ambitious wish. He stamped the snow off his boots, straightened his fur hat, and pushed open the door.

"May I help you?" A bright-eyed shop assistant hurried forward. "Ah, yes," she said when Han Tzu gave his name. "The position of caravan leader to the west. Come this way."

Han Tzu followed the assistant. He loved the west,

and he wanted to lead his own expedition to the lands beyond China's frontier. No longer a camel driver, nor even the camel master in charge of the animals and drivers, he would be the caravan leader. He would hire the men, decide the route, trade at the markets, and bring everyone safely home again.

The shop assistant stood aside. Han Tzu took off his hat and brushed back his soft, black hair. Then he stepped into a room full of treasures. Bolts of silk shimmered on the shelves, and bronze leopards inlaid with gold prowled the table tops. Huge, spiral seashells spilled from wide wicker baskets. At the far end of the room, a frail man with a wispy beard sat on a low sofa. "Come in," Yin Li said. Han Tzu bowed and took a seat on a nearby chair.

"A friend of mine," Yin Li began, "a very careful merchant, has told me that you're an excellent trader. For the last year, you've led his expeditions to the south and brought back great profits. I'd like to know more. Tell me about yourself."

"I was sixteen when I was drafted into the emperor's army," Han Tzu said. He pushed back the folds of his cape and made himself more comfortable. "My unit was sent to keep order in the conquered territories to the west. Every village had its marketplace, and I liked to stop and watch our Chinese traders sell silk to the local people, the ones called barbarians. The Chinese merchants took an interest in me. They taught me

what to buy and how to bargain.

"After I left the army, I joined a caravan as a camel driver. I traveled to Merv and Fergana, the cities beyond the frontier. On each trip, I moved up the ranks. Last year I led my first caravan to the south."

"I expected a much older man." Yin Li studied Han Tzu. "You don't look more than twenty. Too young for what I need." He turned and minutely adjusted a narrow scroll and a bronze money box on the table beside him. The interview appeared to be over.

Han Tzu began talking. He would not let his golden chance slip away. He spoke about his knowledge of the western deserts and mountains. He reviewed the foreign markets and his fluency in the barbarian languages. He laid out the types of goods he could buy, the qualities he looked for in the men he hired, the skill he had in selling at a profit.

"A question," Yin Li held up a pale, blue-veined hand. "The trip to the west is long and difficult. Do you have a family? Will you cut short your trading for an early return?"

Did he have a family? Han Tzu stiffened. In an instant, he saw his father's farm. He was crossing the dirt courtyard, while his parents, his older sisters, and his younger brothers clustered at the family's small stone altar. His brothers lit an offering to their ancestors and fanned the smoke toward the heavens. The prayers for the dead rose in his father's steady chant.

Only his mother cried. Han Tzu reached the edge of the family compound and tugged at the old bamboo gate. It creaked open, but his family never glanced over. For them he no longer existed. He swung his pack to his shoulder, looked back one last time, and stepped out onto the road.

Han Tzu shook his head. "No. I don't have a family."

Yin Li changed the subject. "What do you know about Parthia?"

Han Tzu rubbed his palms against his woolen trousers. The rough cloth reassured him. "The capital, Merv, is not very big, but its goods are amazing. In the market, I've seen birds with tails that fan into rainbows and stilt-legged geese with necks and heads way above my own. The gems are like sparks of fire."

"Have you gone beyond Merv?" Yin Li's gaze grew intense.

"No," Han Tzu said. "The Parthians block the way. They keep the trade routes through their empire to themselves."

"I've heard that the Parthians take our silk across their own kingdom and sell it to other traders. These new merchants then carry the silk farther west—to a city at the end of the world."

"It's true," Han Tzu said, leaning forward. "I've heard that the people in this city have wild yellow or red hair, and their eyes are often as green as the sea or

as blue as the sky. They're all wealthy, and they pay enormous sums for silk."

Yin Li sat back. "I envy you. I'd travel west, but my age and business keep me here. Instead, you'll go for me." He reached for the scroll on the table, unrolled it, and read off a list of trade goods. "I'm sending silk, bronze mirrors, jade figures, and lacquerware to Merv. You'll sell them and buy gold, raw jade, rugs, and gems. The trip out should last about three months. On the way back, stop in Fergana and buy the spirited horses that our nobles crave. When you return, about nine months from now, I'll sell these goods, and you'll be paid handsomely."

Yin Li rerolled the scroll and lifted seven cords of coins out of the small, bronze money box. Each coin was round with a square hole in the middle. "Five strands are for buying supplies. The rest are half your wages."

Han Tzu allowed himself a quick smile. The caravan to Merv was actually his. He took the bronze coins, slipped them into his leather pouch, and tucked the scroll under his belt. He made a deep bow. The interview had ended, and he was eager to get started.

Chapter 2

Outside Yin Li's shop, the deep boom of a drum announced that the marketplace had opened. Han Tzu slipped into the throng of soldiers, shoppers, and thieves streaming toward the bazaar. Soon the rhythm of buying supplies absorbed him completely.

Each purchase brought the caravan to Merv closer. The new baskets would hold patterned rugs and bright silks. Stiff leather harnesses would help control the camels, and huge copper pots would hold stew to warm the travelers on cold desert nights. The thought of food brought him back to the present. He was hungry. If he hurried, he might find lunch and the cook he wanted to hire at the same tavern.

Off a nearby alley, Han Tzu entered a narrow, smoky

restaurant. By the door, a table of merchants devoured plates of fish and pickled vegetables. A cluster of soldiers laughed, tipped back their chairs, and shouted for more wine. Across the room, peasants at a long table noisily slurped their soup. One of them, a heavy man with a thick neck and a bald head, looked up. Han Tzu recognized Wei Chien. "I thought I might find you here," he said.

"Come join us." Wei Chien waved him over. "We're just beginning." Han Tzu grabbed a stool, and Wei Chien introduced his sister, two brothers, a nephew, and several cousins. Then he rushed through the names of a dozen neighbors and friends from his village.

"Are you a merchant in Changan?" Wei Chien's sister asked wide-eyed.

"No. I'm a caravan leader and a trader." Han Tzu waited for her reaction. Wei Chien's sister and all his other relatives and friends registered this information in silence. Then one after another their expressions turned from interest to mistrust.

"Barbarians? You spend your time among barbarians?" Wei Chien's cousin, a thin, pinched man, let his sharp voice rise until his question sounded like an accusation.

"I hear they don't worship their ancestors," a plump woman said softly to the young man across the table. He nodded, and she shot a glance at Han Tzu.

"Someone told me," a man in a faded brown cap

said, as if he had seen it for himself, "that barbarians never plow or sow crops. They've no statues or family altars. Instead, they wander about without homes or fields."

"Traders aren't much better," an old man added.

"That's right," a young woman spoke up. "Traders never settle down. They buy our goods for nothing, triple the prices, and sell them at the next market. We're the ones who sweat, while they take all the profit."

The table went wild. The villagers shouted and waved their hands. They told stories of barbarians who lived unnatural lives and of traders who cheated and stole from honest folk.

"Enough!" Wei Chien rose from his seat and pounded on the rough table. The soup splashed. The soldiers and merchants looked up. "Han Tzu is honest," Wei Chien said. "Eat your meal and leave him alone." The cook sat down again, and the bench groaned. Unconvinced but silenced, the villagers went back to their lunch.

Han Tzu was dismayed. He'd heard all these outlandish stories before, but they still stung. The morning's happiness drained away. Still he had an expedition to organize. "Yin Li wants me to form a caravan," he said to Wei Chien. "I'll need a cook. Will you come with me to Parthia?"

"Can we stop in Fergana?" Wei Chien asked, his spoon in midair. "The farmers there grow the most

delicious fruit—shiny red globes called apples. Of course, we might die of thirst in the desert or be buried by a mountain avalanche before we even arrive." He paused and looked somber. Then his eyes twinkled. "But it's been years since I've had a crisp, fresh apple. I'll come."

"Good," Han Tzu said. "We'll stop in Fergana on the way back."

"Wait," Wei Chien wagged his spoon. "I'll need an assistant. One that I choose. And you'll advance me the money to buy the food." Han Tzu smiled. Wei Chien was not only a fine cook but also a bossy, opinionated man.

"We'll need flour, dried fish, pickled vegetables, meat, syrup, relishes, dried beans, and salt. Sour oranges are expensive, so we'll take only a dozen baskets. They'll keep, and we can trade or sell them for more supplies." Wei Chien reached for a dumpling. A quick swallow and he continued. "I'll bring drinks in large, leather pouches. Along the route, we'll buy more drinks, summer fruits, wild game, and barley."

Han Tzu's stomach knotted at the thought of the caravan's food bill. Then he remembered that he still hadn't eaten. He waved over a serving boy, ordered a meal, and let his mind drift with Wei Chien's chatter. He had accomplished enough for one morning.

Chapter 3

The next day, at the silk merchant's shop, Han Tzu
pushed his way through the customers to the front of
the crowd. He drummed his fingers lightly on the
counter and waited for help. A half-folded screen separated the shop from a room at the back, where he
could see a young woman working at a large loom.
She sat in front of a length of fine blue threads. Her
small feet pressed the pedals, and the threads opened.
Her wrist flicked, and a spool of blue silk skimmed
along the fibers. She caught the shuttle and pulled the
comblike beater toward her. With a whoosh, the
beater pressed the new thread into the fabric.

"Good morning, sir," the shop owner said to Han
Tzu. "What can I do for you?"

"I've come to pick up an order of silk for the merchant Yin Li."

The short, round shopkeeper stepped onto a wooden ladder and pulled bolts of cloth from a high shelf. Waves of deep blue, scarlet, gold, and silver tumbled onto the counter.

"Yin Li ordered wisely," the shop owner said from his perch. "Here are his bolts with the embroidered dragons for good fortune. Over there are the ones with the gold and silver inlays. Look at these bolts. See how the patterns stand away from the background. The clouds are scrolls along the border of the fabric, and the pattern of diamonds and checks has been woven into the cloth. Everything is just as he wished."

Han Tzu touched the fabrics with his callused fingers. Some silks were airy, others heavy. He recalled the legend of the discovery of silk. Long ago on a spring day, the empress Hsi Ling-Shi sat in her garden under the shade of a mulberry tree. A cocoon from a branch of the tree fell into her cup of tea and unraveled into a single, delicate thread. Delighted, she ordered garments woven from the strand.

"Will there be something else?" the shopkeeper asked.

"I'd like to see something for my own trading." Han Tzu nodded toward the workroom. He always took something of his own to sell. It made him feel that the journey was for himself as well as for his employer.

The owner bowed and pulled aside the screen.

"Perhaps this might do," the shop owner said. He motioned for Han Tzu to come over to the loom of blue silk. "Here is the weaving of my wife, Wu Mei. Her silk looks plain, but I assure you, when it's finished, it will be warm and soft and fall in perfect folds. It's not a large bolt, just enough for two long robes. But there's plenty of fabric for wide, square sleeves and a high collar. I guarantee any noble would be proud to wear a coat of this silk."

The shop owner waited expectantly. Han Tzu looked at the smooth, even cloth. From where he stood, it shimmered with a life of its own.

"How do you make it so beautiful?" Han Tzu asked the weaver.

Wu Mei reached out and stroked the strands on the loom. "Memory," she said. She looked past him. "This silk is the blue feathery down on the lake ducklings. It's the blue streams fed by fresh snow and the palest petals of the spring iris." She paused. "When you look at it, what do you remember?"

Han Tzu half-closed his eyes. The silk was the color of the sky at sunrise. How many times had he watched for that color at the end of a long night in the desert? The first blue of the morning sky gave him energy. It made him stronger and more confident.

"Will you take the silk?" the shopkeeper broke into his thoughts.

Han Tzu squared his shoulders. "Yes. I'll take it. I'll sell it to a man I know in Merv."

"A wise decision," the owner said. "You'll make a handsome profit."

The blue silk would be ready in ten days. Han Tzu bundled Yin Li's bolts under his cape. At the shop door, he glanced back. Wu Mei was seated at the loom, weaving his silk. He'd made the right decision.

Chapter 4

ook what you've done! You've spilled everything!"
Han Tzu heard the shouts as he crossed the stable
courtyard. A month had passed since his first meeting with Yin Li, and the morning of departure had finally arrived. In a corner of the courtyard, Wei Chien
stood in the back of a wooden wagon. A young man
on the ground picked up a jumble of ladles and
wooden bowls and put them back in a large wicker
basket.

"Break my knives, I'll break your head," Wei Chien
promised. "If we starve in the desert, it'll be your
fault." The cook passed a bulging leather pouch to the
young man, then a basket of oranges, followed by a
crate of squawking chickens.

Han Tzu headed for the wagon. "Good morning, Wei Chien. I'm happy to see you've found an assistant."

Wei Chien put down a sack of rice and jumped off the cart. "My nephew, Wei Po," the cook said with a careless wave. "My brother says he can't keep a pig in a pen, and he's all mine. From his work this morning, I'm not sure I want him."

Han Tzu studied the boy. Wei Po had his uncle's broad forehead and wide cheeks. He lacked the cook's big belly, but he was as tall and as strong as Wei Chien.

"Don't be too hard on him," Han Tzu said. "Once he gets used to the routine, he'll be fine. Besides, you've probably scared him already with your stories about the desert." Wei Po looked up and nodded.

Wei Chien climbed back on the wagon. Han Tzu started toward the stables, but he could hear Wei Chien lecturing his nephew. "Don't look to Han Tzu for sympathy. I'm the one who makes your dinner. Now catch this bundle."

Had he made a mistake? A doubt crossed Han Tzu's mind. On a long trip, a blustering, cantankerous cook could keep the men in good spirits. But the same man could also be headstrong. Would he be able to control Wei Chien? He entered the stables.

"Show me the animals," Han Tzu said to the wiry man at the open door.

The camel master had purchased the animals for the

expedition and had hired the drivers. With a shy smile, he led the way to the rough stalls. The two-humped animals, not much taller than the camel master, munched on the hay in their feed troughs. "See how fat their humps are?" he said. "They have all the food they'll need to cross the desert."

Han Tzu ran his hand along the animals' sides and caught his fingers in the long, soft hair of their winter coats. The hollow behind their ribs was only a slight indentation. During the journey their humps and sides would shrink as they used up the fat stored in their bodies.

Han Tzu stopped next to one of the mares and held out his palm. A young foal pressed its soft, gray muzzle into his open hand. "How old is this little fellow?"

"He was born just two weeks ago." The stern camel master looked pleased. "But he's ready to travel."

Han Tzu ordered the animals brought outside and loaded. He walked about the courtyard and said a few words to each driver. Near the gate, Wei Po struggled to balance the baskets on his camel. Han Tzu double-checked the baskets on his own mount.

The fastening on one pack was loose, so he un-knotted the rope and peered inside. Brightly decorated lacquered bowls filled the top. Under them lay the bundles of gleaming silk. His own blue bolt was tucked safe and snug among the other fabrics. It was exactly the right shade. He reclosed the basket and

tied a tight knot. His heart was pounding, a familiar sign. It was time to leave.

While a stable hand held the bridle, Han Tzu swung into the saddle and urged his camel up. He took the reins in one hand and waved his other arm high over his head. "Let's go!" He pointed toward the courtyard entrance. At once the yard was awash with noise and movement. Drivers shouted. Camels spit and stamped. They churned the ground, damp from recent rains and animal droppings, into a sea of mud.

Like a string unrolling from a ball, sixty men, their mounts, and thirty pack animals strung themselves single file out of the stable compound. Almost the last animal to leave was the mare. Close behind on strong but spindly legs trotted her young foal.

By midmorning the heavy traffic on the main road thinned, and Changan gave way to farms. Han Tzu could see that spring planting had begun. Families bent in the fields and turned over the damp brown soil with wooden hoes. He, too, had once knelt in the furrows, crumbled apart the soft earth, and pushed in the oval seeds.

Han Tzu had returned from the army eager to be a farmer again, and his family had met him with outstretched arms. At first he was content, but in less than a year his thoughts turned to travel. He daydreamed about faraway cities and talked about exotic goods and foreign markets. He tried to explain the

thrill of bargaining. His sisters clucked. His brothers ignored him. He argued that they could learn something, but they tapped their heads.

"You've been bewitched," his older sister said. "You're not the brother we once knew."

"A trader is a demon," his favorite brother said. "Our crops will fail because of your stories."

His mother followed him to the fields, her eyes red-rimmed and sad. "Please. Say you'll stop this talk."

"Be silent," his father commanded, "or become a trader. If you join the caravans, have no doubt, we will forget you." His brothers agreed. Only his mother pleaded with him to stay. In the end, Han Tzu packed his things and said good-bye.

He gazed at the families in the fields and was envious, lonely, and angry all at the same time. He spurred his camel. The quicker he passed the familiar farms, the sooner he would shake off his unhappy memories.

Chapter 5

Stop in the name of the emperor!" A guard with an iron spear stepped into the middle of the road. The caravan halted at an imperial checkpoint twenty days out of Changan. Han Tzu dismounted and headed for the guardhouse. A checkpoint could be tricky. Sometimes the officials waved a caravan through. Often they detained travelers for hours or even days.

In the little guardhouse, the captain, a stiff man with a thin black mustache, reached for the expedition's documents. He reviewed the travel passes. Once. Then again. Han Tzu's shoulders tensed. Why was it taking so long? All the documents were in order. Still the captain continued to study them.

"Stop! Let him go." Wei Chien's voice broke the

silence. Han Tzu stepped outside to see two guards drag Wei Po off to the side of the road. A third soldier held Wei Chien at swordpoint.

"Leave the boy alone!"

"Mind your own business, fat one," said a guard.

"Ignorant border guards," Wei Chien snorted.

"The boy's a thief, and we're taking him back to Changan."

"He's not a thief. He's my nephew!"

"Wake up, old fool. Even a nephew can commit a crime. Check your own money pouch."

Han Tzu turned to the patrol captain who had followed him out of the guardhouse. "You've orders to arrest Wei Po?"

"We know him to be a thief," the officer said.

Han Tzu studied the struggling boy. Was Wei Po really a thief? Or had the captain arrested him because the regional governor needed a crew of healthy young men for road repairs? If the captain kept Wei Po, Wei Chien would leave the caravan. Han Tzu would have to return to Changan for a new cook.

Back in the city, some—perhaps all—of the camel drivers would decide the expedition was jinxed and quit. Yin Li would be furious at the loss of time and money. He'd fire Han Tzu. His first caravan to the west, the expedition of his dreams, would end in disaster.

"Wei Chien seems to care a lot for his nephew," Han Tzu said to the captain. "Of course, I've just met the

boy myself. He's not too bright and not a very good worker. He'll probably eat more than he's worth." Slowly, as he wondered out loud about the value of ignorant villagers, Han Tzu reached into his leather pouch and pulled out a fistful of coins. He jingled them in his hand. "Wei Po must be one of hundreds of peasant boys who pass this way." He let his voice trail off while the heavy coins rubbed and clinked together.

The captain sighed. "You're right, my friend. We shouldn't be too hasty. Boys his age all look alike. Wait in the guardhouse while I talk to my soldiers. They often act without thinking." The captain put his arm around Han Tzu. The two men turned away, and Han Tzu emptied his coins into the officer's open hand.

Later, back on his camel, with Wei Po restored to the caravan, Han Tzu mulled over the incident. Was it a sign of bad luck? He glanced around. The countryside seemed at peace. The camels behind him swayed with their shifting gait. Nothing was out of place. He could relax for now.

Late one afternoon, a little more than a month into the journey, Han Tzu squinted toward the horizon and recognized the faint line of the Great Wall. Here at the edge of the empire, the wall stretched for hundreds of miles interrupted only by watchtowers staffed by army units. These garrisons protected Chinese towns and villages from invasion by the western tribes. The caravan hurried its pace. When it was within hailing

distance, soldiers at the Great Wall hurried out, several shouting at once.

"Welcome!"

"What news? Are you from Changan?"

"How long have you been away?"

"Come in, come in. You're our first visitors this spring."

The garrison commander, a hardened soldier with a slight limp, emerged from his quarters. When he saw Han Tzu, his lined face broke into a smile. "What a pleasure. You're back again," he said. "It's been two years, hasn't it? Of course, you'll stay the night as my special guest."

Han Tzu was flattered. Lu Tan was a brave soldier who had served for decades at the wall, and he always had stories to tell. "The caravan's going to Merv," Han Tzu said. He tried not to draw attention to the fact that he was the leader.

"So, you're in charge this time." Lu Tan noticed everything. "Well, now we have something special to celebrate. Let me show you to your room, and later you'll join me for dinner. We'll talk about old times, and you can tell me about your expedition." Smoke rose from the garrison kitchen. Han Tzu smelled roast mutton. He forgot his fatigue and followed Lu Tan inside.

The next morning, before a very early breakfast, Han Tzu climbed up to the watchtower. He wanted a few moments to himself. On the roof, he crossed to the

rough stone parapet that faced west. This was the world he craved. Today he would lead his caravan across the border and out into the world beyond China. For a moment, he drank in the shadowy hills, then an eagerness, an urgency to be off, chased away his reflections. He strode back to the ladder.

With one hand on the wooden frame, he glanced down at the empty courtyard. A figure darted out of a doorway. Han Tzu recognized Wei Chien. The cook scuttled crablike across the dusty square with his body bent double and his arms tightly wrapped around a bulky object.

Trouble. Nothing but trouble. Han Tzu started down the ladder. This had to stop. The courtyard was empty, but he knew where to go. He reached the stables just as Wei Chien came barreling out.

The two almost collided. Han Tzu grabbed the front of Wei Chien's shirt and forced him back against the courtyard wall. The cook sagged under his grip and began to babble explanations.

"Shut up." Han Tzu moved his hand onto Wei Chien's throat and squeezed. "You lied, didn't you?" Wei Chien's mouth dropped open, and he panted for breath.

"Wei Po's hiding in the stable because he really is a thief." Wei Chien rolled his eyes toward the stable door as if he could check on the boy hidden behind the hay bales. "And you're bringing him a nice hot breakfast,"

Han Tzu said. Wei Chien nodded feverishly.

"Do you know the danger you've put me in?" Han Tzu didn't wait to hear an answer. "Do you think this commander can be bribed like the border captain? If Lu Tan catches Wei Po, he won't bother to send him back to Changan. He'll cut off his hands here in the courtyard. I'll be fined for harboring a thief, and we won't be allowed to cross the border. The expedition will be finished. My reputation will be ruined."

Han Tzu squeezed a little harder. Beneath the folds of soft flesh, his fingers found Wei Chien's delicate windpipe. He longed to throttle the squirming cook. Instead, he flung him to the ground. "Keep Wei Po out of sight. I don't want to see either of you until we're in the desert." Han Tzu spun on his heel and walked back to his room.

In the courtyard three hours later, Han Tzu mingled among his men and animals. His caravan was loaded, and his drivers rested. He mounted his camel and said his final thanks to Lu Tan. At the commander's signal, pairs of soldiers grabbed the iron rungs on the garrison's heavy wooden gates and pulled them open. His heart racing, Han Tzu led the caravan out of the compound and onto the road leading to the Western Regions.

Chapter 6

Han Tzu savored the morning sun on his back as the caravan moved along the crowded road. Ahead of him, a bright stroke of orange flashed among the muted clothes of the villagers. He spurred his camel and dismounted beside a solitary traveler dressed in the deep saffron robe and simple sandals of a Buddhist monk.

For a few moments, the two men walked in silence. Little clouds of fine dust swirled around their feet. The monk spoke first.

"Once," he began in a low, even voice, "there was a handsome, wealthy prince called Siddhartha Gautama, prince of the Sakyas. His father tried to shield him from all forms of suffering, but the gods drew the

young man out into the world. They showed him poverty, sickness, and death. Siddhartha wanted to find a way to help people. So he left his family and wandered for years, meditating and going without food. In a moment of supreme meditation, he understood the truth and became the Buddha, the Enlightened One."

Han Tzu started to ask a question, but the monk took up the story again. "He met people everywhere who believed that the body died, but the soul returned to earth to live one unhappy life after another. To these people, the Buddha explained that only a life free of too much pain or pleasure could end the cycle of rebirth and give the soul eternal rest."

"And the Buddha?" Han Tzu asked, "Did he ever return to his family?"

The monk paused and looked at Han Tzu for the first time. "Yes, the Buddha returned home, but only because his father wished to see him."

"Your own family?" Han Tzu hesitated. "Can you go home?"

"Try to let go," the monk said. "Nothing stays the same. Everything changes. Let go of all earthly relations, and your soul will reach eternal peace. These are the teachings of the Buddha."

Han Tzu couldn't speak. He would never be called home. His eyes burned, and he had no more questions. He managed a brief good-bye, then he rode

ahead to his caravan.

Nine days beyond the Great Wall, Han Tzu halted his men and animals beside Lop Nor, the marsh on the edge of the Western Regions. He faced a choice of routes around the desert. Over the years, he'd waited and watched as other caravan leaders had made this decision. They had not always chosen wisely. Once a blizzard had engulfed his caravan on the northern route. Another time wells had been dry along the southern track. Either way a caravan could be led off course by a sandstorm. Its members could die of thirst in the Taklimakan Desert, the "Place of No Return." Han Tzu shifted on his camel.

The barren mudflats gave him no clue. He breathed in the air. It was dry and full of sunshine. The camel master and the men were looking at him, waiting for a decision.

He was head of the expedition, and the lives of his men depended on his choice. He was both wary and proud. Briskly, he smacked the side of his camel and pointed to the right. "We'll go north."

The days in the desert stretched from one to three to five to ten. Han Tzu scoured the route. Every twelve-hour day was different. First the track was gravel, then sand, and then gravel again. Animal skeletons, picked bare by vultures and bleached by the sun, lay as landmarks along the way. Day after day passed in a lulling routine.

Late one afternoon, hours before the evening stop, Han Tzu's camel became restless, tossed her head, and tried to turn off the track. She stopped and plunged her neck downward toward the sand. Behind her the other camels brayed and trumpeted. The wind rose.

"Sandstorm!" Han Tzu turned in his saddle and signaled the camel master behind him. Years ago his first sandstorm had caught his military unit at night. He had been on sentry duty, away from camp. In the total darkness, he had stumbled about looking for cover. The winds had howled and pulled at him. They had become voices that mocked and called his name. Waves of rough sand and small stones had battered his head and body until he'd fallen, sobbing, to the ground. The memory still made him shiver.

Han Tzu checked to be sure his men had on their cloaks, and then he quickly wrapped his own nose and mouth in a thick hood. The wind hit with violent, stinging force. He huddled over his animal and let the sharp pebbles fall like blows on his back. Surrounded by swirling sand, he felt alone.

The wind dropped. The hail of small stones ceased, and a powerful, intense silence filled the desert. A few of the camels raised their heads and snorted. Han Tzu pulled off his hood, brushed the sand from his shoulders, and looked around.

The animals were shaking their long necks, while the men dusted off their clothing. With his hand as a

shade, Han Tzu searched for the little foal. There he was. The youngster had pressed himself against his mother's side. Now he took a few cautious steps on his own. He was fine.

Han Tzu ran his tongue over his lips and found they were cracked. He reached for his water bag and took a small sip, rinsed his mouth, and spat out the sand. A new world lay before him. The faint hard track along the desert floor was gone. In its place stretched a smooth blanket of sand marked only by a pattern of long, overlapping ripples. On his left, a huge dune rose where a row of slim trees had stood before the storm. Ahead the sun hung just a little lower in the western sky.

Together Han Tzu and the camel master took fresh bearings. The men and animals moved into formation and once more began to cross the desert.

Chapter 7

 ot and spicy! Fit for the emperor! Quick now, before I eat it all." Wei Chien banged the bottom of a metal pan and called the men to supper. The caravan had traveled its daily thirty miles, and Han Tzu had ordered a stop at a small oasis.

The men crowded into a ragged line, and Wei Chien ladled a steaming stew into their lacquered bowls. They settled themselves around the campfire. Wei Po moved among them, offering the leather pouches and fresh camel's milk from a brass pitcher. The little foal was thriving, and his mother gave milk for him and the men.

"Want some more?" Wei Chien served Han Tzu.

"No, thanks. This is fine." Relations between the

two men were polite but cool.

"Bring out your flute, One Eye," Wei Chien said to a half-blind camel driver. Some of the men had finished their meal and had unrolled their sleeping mats to stretch out around the fire.

"And the drum, too," the camel master said to an older musician.

"Play a tune that reminds us of home," Wei Chien said. He glanced slyly at his nephew. "Play something for Wei Po. He's got a sweetheart. Play him a song about love." The cook rested his bald head against Wei Po's shoulder and sighed like a young girl.

Wei Po pushed his uncle away, and the men laughed. On the edge of the circle, Han Tzu smiled, too. Wei Chien teased everyone, but he was very careful not to mock the caravan leader.

"Join us at *lio po?*" the camel master asked.

"Not tonight." Han Tzu glanced at the game board and the cup with small bamboo rods as dice. "I lost too much last time." He stood up and shook his stiff legs. "I'm going to plot our position."

Out on the wide, black plateau, he looked back. The campsite was a hearth of glowing embers. The sounds of the flute and drum drifted up into the inky sky. How small his caravan seemed under the cold stars. Yet each day he led it deeper into a country that most men feared to enter.

Later that night, the sky clouded over, and the winds

blew in short, shifting blasts. Han Tzu tossed in a sleep so light that when the sand crunched, he sat bolt upright. Wei Chien hurried toward him.

"He's gone," Wei Chien said, his eyes darting into the night. "Ever since the sandstorm, Wei Po's had nightmares. The demons of the desert call to him. They promise him pleasures. They threaten and torment him. He walks in his sleep. Now he's under their spell, and they'll never give him up."

Han Tzu followed Wei Chien to the empty, rumpled bedroll near the campfire. "How long has he been gone?"

"I don't know, but I'll find him." Wei Chien flung a blanket around his shoulders and headed away from the camp.

"Come back!" Han Tzu caught up with the stumbling cook. "Build a fire while I ride out." He untied one of the camels, slipped onto his back, and rode south. The campfire blazed behind him, then grew smaller as he moved farther away.

Darkness closed in. The wind hissed and moaned. Dry twigs flew up. They tapped at his leg, poked at his back. He whipped around. No one was there.

Hours passed. Han Tzu looked back toward the fire. It still burned brightly. His hopes of finding Wei Po were dwindling, but he dreaded going back without him. Would Wei Chien miss his nephew and feel the same loneliness that haunted Han Tzu? Surely he

would. Han Tzu urged his camel onward. He couldn't bear to bring anyone such sadness.

He headed toward the heart of the desert. The wind dropped away, and the clouds melted from black to pearl gray. The palest line of blue appeared between the night sky and the earth. For the first time in weeks, Han Tzu remembered the blue silk.

He turned his camel toward the east. In his mind's eye, he compared his silk with the sky. Fresh and clean, they were an exact match. He moved toward the horizon. The sky became rosy, and bursts of orange shot into the band of blue. Over a small hill and almost out of sight of the campfire, his camel shied to the left. At the same moment, a cry broke from the rocks. Half-hidden in a stony hollow was the crumpled figure of the sleepwalker Wei Po.

When Han Tzu returned with the boy, he found Wei Chien adding herbs to a bubbling broth. The cook gently lifted Wei Po down, wrapped him in blankets, and cradled him in his arms. Little by little, he spooned the soup into him. Wei Po swallowed the broth and then slept. Wei Chien sat nearby, patting his nephew's shoulder at his slightest stir.

The men gathered round. "He's a fine boy, a bit too serious, but a hard worker."

"The demons of the desert chose him because he's the youngest."

"Yes, that's right. He's lucky to be alive."

"When he wakes up, he won't remember what he saw or did last night. The demons will have blotted out his memory."

"Move away. Let him rest." Han Tzu broke into the circle. He watched the sleeping boy. Now that Wei Po had been found, he felt a strange kind of happiness. He had to admit it. Wei Chien and Wei Po were important to him. They were the heart of his caravan.

Han Tzu stretched to shake off his fatigue. "Load up the animals," he said to his men. "Tie Wei Po behind Wei Chien with a blanket. His uncle's as good as a soft bed." The sun was up. It was time to travel.

Chapter 8

Han Tzu brought the expedition into the oasis of Kucha a month and a half out of Changan and about twenty days after his stop at the Great Wall. The village was the halfway point in his journey. He was right on time.

The next day, the village elder, his wife, and a noisy party of small children invited Han Tzu, the camel master, and Wei Chien to dinner. Wei Chien insisted on bringing Wei Po. The men seated themselves on rugs around a low central table. From a large cauldron, the women served thick chunks of meat in a fragrant sauce.

"What are we eating?" Wei Po asked his uncle quietly.

Wei Chien closed his eyes and concentrated. "Yak

stew in mare's milk. Delicious."

"It's very good," Han Tzu said to the chief's wife. Her large gold earrings brushed against her cheeks as she poured him a fresh cup of fermented mare's milk. One of the serving women had taken a special fancy to Wei Chien, and she made sure his leather cup was never empty.

"Come. Let us dance." The village elder stood up and clapped his hands. The women and younger boys cleared away the table. Several men brought out stringed instruments, and others gathered in the center of the room. A slow circle dance began. Han Tzu retreated to watch from a bench along the wall.

"Wait for me," Wei Chien hurried to a place in the circle. He swayed in time to the raspy music. He shuffled his feet and stepped left. Everyone else stepped right. The villagers turned once. Wei Chien turned twice. He invented new steps, sang out of tune, and when the music stopped, made a deep bow. Wei Po took his uncle by the elbow and led him to a seat. Wei Chien called for more mare's milk. Two cups later, he was back among the dancers.

Well after midnight, the travelers said their good-byes and headed back to camp. Halfway to the oasis, Wei Chien began to sing at the top of his voice. He tripped and stumbled along the path, imitating the dignified dancing of the village chief.

"We should have left while he could still walk

straight," Han Tzu said. Wei Po didn't answer. His uncle had flung one arm around his shoulders. Wei Po staggered to keep Wei Chien upright.

"Here, let me help you." Han Tzu pulled Wei Chien's other arm over his own shoulder. Together the two men half-dragged, half-led the sleepy cook back to camp. They rolled him onto his mat, threw a blanket over him, and left him to snore. Han Tzu poked at the campfire. A few coals broke into flame, and he settled himself by the embers. Wei Po joined him.

"I must thank you," Wei Po said, "for finding me in the desert."

Han Tzu looked up, surprised. Once or twice, he had given Wei Po an order or asked him a question, but he had never talked with him. "Don't worry, the desert makes people do strange things. I'm just glad we found you."

"My uncle is also grateful, even though he tries not to show it."

"He certainly saves his kind words," Han Tzu said.

"Oh, it's just the way he is." Wei Po shrugged. "I think he really does care."

Han Tzu was surprised at Wei Po's insight. A question struck him, and he was fairly sure that he could ask it.

"What did you steal?"

"I didn't steal anything."

The warmth of the conversation sputtered like the

fire, but Han Tzu wasn't ready to let it go out. He threw another bundle of twigs on the coals, and the orange flames licked at the new tinder.

"Well, what happened?" Han Tzu asked. "Something must have happened. The checkpoint patrol had your name, and Wei Chien hid you at the Great Wall."

Wei Po stretched out his hands before the fire. "In our village, I worked as a swineherd for the local landowner. He lived alone and had hundreds of animals, while we had big families and only a few hens. One night his prize pig followed me home."

"Followed you home?"

"Well, yes," he said with a sigh. "Little bits of his favorite mushroom fell out of my hand. Of course, it was my fault that I forgot to lock his pen, but I never stole the pig."

"And then?"

"And then," Wei Po spoke slowly as if trying to remember some long-ago event, "when the pig got to our village, he walked by Wei Chien who was sharpening his ax."

Han Tzu tried not to smile at the image of a prize pig parading through the middle of a small, muddy village. "What happened next?"

"Hard to tell." Wei Po looked puzzled. "Probably my uncle was so surprised that he dropped the ax on the pig."

Han Tzu could hardly believe his ears. Wei Chien

not only knew that his nephew was guilty, but he had helped to commit the crime.

"In the end," Wei Po said, "everyone ate a big supper. At dawn our neighbors hid us under a wagonload of winter squash and took us to Changan. I think I met you at the inn that day. You were looking for a cook. You offered Wei Chien the job, and he told me I could come as his assistant."

Han Tzu remembered that Wei Chien had said something about needing an assistant. The cook had tricked him into providing an escape for Wei Po. For a moment, he was angry, but then he just shook his head. "All right. Your secret's safe with me."

The mare's milk had finally made Han Tzu sleepy. He stood up, yawned, and walked over to his mat. Wei Po continued to sit, a dark triangle before the fire. Next to him, his uncle was a small, rounded mountain. Han Tzu chuckled. They were a clever pair.

After several days of trading, Han Tzu said farewell to the villagers of Kucha and headed his caravan back onto the desert route. Several weeks of travel passed without incident. Then one afternoon, a little more than two months after he had left Changan, Han Tzu saw before him the towering heights of the Pamir Mountains. The caravan started up the narrow trail.

At the highest valley, the Pass of Poplars, the air became thinner. Han Tzu could hardly breathe. A metal band seemed strapped around his chest, and each

breath tightened it another notch. The cold air hurt his lungs.

The camel master stepped up. "The men are faint," he said. His words came out with an effort. "They have headaches, and their noses bleed constantly. Our animals are slowing down. They're gasping for breath."

"I know," Han Tzu said. "My head is pounding, too. Tell the men to walk and spare the animals. Tell them anyone who can't walk will be left behind."

The trail was steep and uneven. Each day the camels trudged slower and slower. At one point, they refused to go farther and simply stood panting on the trail.

Han Tzu called to the drivers, "Get out your knives."

The exhausted drivers nodded and moved along the narrow ledge. They gripped the camels' heads by the harnesses and raised their glinting blades. Carefully they slit the camels' nostrils. The bright red blood flowed onto the spring snow. Freed from the pressure in their ears, the animals began to move again. The cuts would heal within the next few days.

Just when Han Tzu thought he and his men could no longer bear the pain, they arrived at the summit. "We made it," the camel master gasped.

The one-eyed camel driver hugged Wei Chien. The drummer gave Wei Po a single pat on the back. Some of the men slumped against their animals. Others rewarded themselves with a drink of water.

Han Tzu gazed at the mountain range that stretched below him. He raised his arms as if to embrace all that he saw. Before him wave after snow-covered wave rolled to the blue horizon.

Behind Han Tzu, the party had begun the descent. The little foal, now a sturdy youngster, moved nimbly ahead of his mother. With a last look, Han Tzu turned to follow. His camel picked her way down the mountains, and the treeless slopes yielded to dense forest. His head cleared, and he took deep breaths. The caravan had finally reached Parthia.

Chapter 9

Three and a half months after he'd left Changan, Han Tzu made his way through the crowded market-place at Merv. The days were at their longest, and the eager merchants stayed open into the evening hours. They shouted to him in a mixture of Persian and Chinese, inviting him to buy ostrich eggs, leopards, and slaves. Han Tzu waved them away.

He was looking for a certain Parthian merchant. The man had a little boy and a shop with a parrot in a bright brass cage. Han Tzu remembered that the boy was always in and out of the shop, looking for his toys, running to join his friends. Near the end of his last trip, Han Tzu had given the child a good-luck charm, a small jade bear on a leather thong.

Han Tzu heard a shout. A thin boy of about eleven waved him over. "Yes, Father, it's really the same man. I know it's him," the boy said.

Vardanes, the merchant, looked uncertain, "How can you be so sure, Pacorus? You were very young."

"Not so young. Look. Here's the charm he gave me." Pacorus took a jade bear on a leather thong out of his shirt. Han Tzu pointed at the bear and nodded his head. Speaking in Persian, Vardanes welcomed him back to Merv.

The trading took almost a month. Each day Han Tzu left the caravansary, the wide, square courtyard of stables and narrow rooms used by travelers, and brought new things to Vardanes's shop. Sometimes he sold only a few items and stayed to talk and feed nuts to Lilli, the boy's parrot. Other days the two men were all business, and nothing distracted them. Gradually, Han Tzu sold everything and restocked his baskets with gems, rugs, and gold to take back to Yin Li. Only the blue silk remained.

On the final morning of trading, Han Tzu stood in the crowded caravansary with the blue silk. The summer sun burned down. In one corner, Wei Chien prepared lunch over a smoky fire. He chopped onions and swatted flies with his square cleaver. "Is that it?" The cook looked up at Han Tzu. "The last bolt, or lacquered pot, or whatever else you have in those bottomless baskets?"

Was it the heat or was Wei Chien anxious to start back? "I'll finish trading this afternoon, and we'll leave in another day or two," Han Tzu said. "Looking forward to going home?"

"Home? I'm never going home. I'll never walk into my own house again." Wei Chien threw the onions into the frying pan, and they sizzled in the hot oil.

Han Tzu stopped short. He'd forgotten that Wei Chien and Wei Po were thieves. They didn't dare return to their village. He was sorry he'd mentioned the return trip, and then he remembered that he couldn't go home either.

He waited for the painful memories. His heart beat steadily. A fly buzzed near his ear. Nothing happened. He deliberately called up the image of his father, his mother, his family in the courtyard. He saw them and he was sad, but the memory didn't hurt the way it had before. The old loneliness was gone. He was free of it, and he wanted to tell someone.

"Well, you're not alone," Han Tzu said. His voice caught. "You're not the only ones who can't go home." His throat cleared. "My family threw me out years ago because I liked trading with barbarians."

Wei Chien dropped his knife and stood up. "Hey, Wei Po. Han Tzu can't go home either. His family has disowned him." Han Tzu winced at the word, even if it was true.

Wei Po left his half-scrubbed pots and came over.

"Well, he can live with us."

"Of course!" Wei Chien said. "Old Pickle-face, our landlady back in Changan, will have a room for you. I'll cook, you'll find us another caravan, and we'll travel together."

"Two pig thieves and a restless trader," Han Tzu said with a smile. "That sounds fine to me." What an unlikely household they'd make. Yet he knew that it would work and that he'd be happy.

Later, seated on the rugs in the back of Vardanes's shop, Han Tzu brought out his blue silk. Vardanes made a generous offer and waited. Han Tzu studied the blue. The color had led him toward the dawn and Wei Po. Without it he wouldn't have found the sleep-walking boy or his new family. But it wasn't practical to keep it. What would he do with it, journey after journey? Reluctantly he accepted Vardanes's price. The bargain was sealed, and Pacorus stacked the cloth on a nearby shelf.

Han Tzu rose to leave. He looked for a final time at the blue silk. What had the weaver, Wu Mei, said? Memory, she'd told him, makes the silk special. The blue is the world you know and love. He would see the silk again, year after year, at sunrise in the desert.

The trading was finished, and Han Tzu began to plan the return trip. He would go to Fergana and buy horses for Yin Li. The caravan would arrive in time for apples and peaches. He imagined blue bowls filled

with red and golden fruits. What would Wei Po think of peaches? Would Wei Chien enjoy his apples?

In late summer, Han Tzu would cross the desert and arrive at the Great Wall in time for the autumn harvest festivals. Before the first snowflakes fell, he would be back at Changan, ready to enter the city gates.

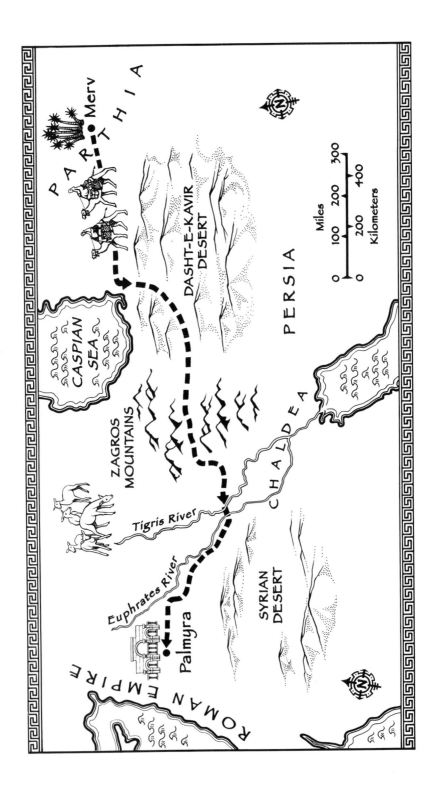

The Blue Silk
Goes from
Merv to Palmyra

Chapter 10

I like him," Pacorus said after Han Tzu had left. "He's nice, and he always brings treats for Lilli." He turned to the brass cage and passed his parrot a nut.

"The man's a sharp trader," Vardanes added. "He can choose the best rug in a matter of minutes. And he drives a hard bargain."

"But he was funny about his blue silk. At first, I thought he wouldn't sell it, but he did. Why did he change his mind?"

Vardanes shrugged. "Wondering never filled the soup pot. Our job is to take the goods to Palmyra."

"Our job?" Pacorus jumped at the word. Once a year, his father joined a caravan of other merchants to travel west to Palmyra, the great city on the border of

Parthia and Rome. Over the years, first his older cousins and then his own friends had set out with their fathers. Even some of the younger boys had made the trip, and still his father had not invited him.

"Can I go this time?" Pacorus tried to keep his voice calm so it wouldn't rise and crack with longing.

Vardanes didn't answer. With deliberate movements, he straightened a lopsided pile of rugs. Lilli fluffed her wings and pecked at the nuts in her cage. Vardanes's eyes sunk deeper, and a little crease formed between his thick, dark brows. Pacorus recognized the look. His father was weighing an offer, turning it over in his mind.

"Seventy merchants are forming a caravan, and they've invited me to join them. They've hired a caravan leader, a guide, and a camel master. The journey is long and dangerous. It's not a trip for a child." Vardanes stopped.

This habit of his father's—to speak, stop, and then speak again—made Pacorus edgy. He was just the opposite. His opinions popped out like rabbits from low bushes. Now he pressed his lips together and covered his mouth with his fist for good measure.

"The most respected men in Parthia are merchants," Vardanes said. "I've always planned for you to join our ranks. So you may come."

"Hurrah!" Pacorus sprang up and tried to touch the ceiling of the shop. He was going to Palmyra. At the

same time, he heard the caution in his father's invitation. 'You may come' was not the same as 'I want you to come.'

"You should also realize," Vardanes warned, "that you'll make many mistakes. But mistakes sometimes teach more than successes do. For this first journey, I'll give you some money. You can buy goods in Palmyra and sell them back here in Merv."

"No, not the money," Pacorus shook his head. "I want something I can trade." No sooner had he spoken than he wanted to take back his words. His father had offered him the trip he longed for, and now he was arguing about it.

"That's a risky way to start, my son," Vardanes said. His eyes darkened. "You could travel to Palmyra and find no customers. Or you could find a buyer but sell your goods at a loss. You'd come home empty-handed, and half a year would've been wasted."

Lilli squawked, and Pacorus glanced at her. A color on her feathers caught his eye, and without a second thought, he said, "May I take the blue silk?"

Vardanes looked surprised. "As you wish. Perhaps there's something special about it. Maybe the silk will bring you good luck."

He would sell the blue silk at a profit in Palmyra. Pacorus knew he would. At the same time, the journey ahead was scary. The men in the market talked about death in the Dasht-e-Kavir Desert and attacks by

robbers in the Zagros Mountains. They also said that as Parthians they were never afraid. They were the link between China and Rome. Without their brave caravans, no silk would ever cross from east to west.

The last evening at home, Pacorus sat in the garden with his younger sister, Susam. For a while, they'd tossed her ball back and forth, but when it rolled into a tangle of sage and violets, they let it go. The silence was awkward. Susam, with all the dignity of her eight years, smoothed her skirt and tightened the red wool bows on her braids.

"Do you have everything?" she said and studied her plait.

"I think so."

"Not everything." Susam tossed back her braid. Pacorus looked at her with a touch of irritation. "You don't have this." She reached into her pocket and brought out a large, woolen square embroidered with animals and red and yellow flowers.

"It's your embroidery!"

"No, it's not."

He was caught once again in Susam's favorite trick. He would think he knew something, but then she would prove him wrong. He would correct himself, but she would announce that he was wrong again. In sheer frustration, Pacorus would ask why she did this. "Older brothers don't know everything," she would remind him. Now she dangled the square in front of him.

"But it's your embroidery! I've seen you—"

"Oh, in the beginning, it might have been," she interrupted, "but now it's something more important. Guess." Pacorus couldn't think.

"It's a pouch! For you." With a flourish Susam shook open the cloth and pushed her hand inside.

"It's very nice." Pacorus was cautious. "But I don't need a pouch."

"Yes, you do. You need it, but you don't even know you need it." Susam's face lit up. "Where are you going to put your blue silk?"

His little sister had tricked him again. She was right. He didn't have a special place to put his silk. His father had asked if he wanted to pack it with the other bolts. Pacorus had said no and had laid it among his own clothes.

"Thank you, Susam," Pacorus said, deciding to be gracious on this last evening. "You're right. I don't have a special pouch." He went to get the cloth. She would never let him rest until she saw that the silk fit perfectly. With a little more folding, it slipped into the bag and was safe and protected. He wouldn't tell her, but he liked the idea of having something she'd made on the trip. He would be less homesick.

On the day of departure, Vardanes and Pacorus said good-bye to the family in the garden. His mother called him "my newest trader." Susam gave him one last bone-crushing hug. His father held his mother's

hands a few extra seconds, and then they were off.
Pacorus started to shout good-bye to every courtyard,
but his father hushed him.

Once out of the city and onto the western route, life
in the caravan settled into a routine. Pacorus was surprised at how many hours the men spent in the saddle.
The caravan followed the old roads that wound between the mountains. Sometimes the merchants met
other expeditions. Occasionally they passed mounted
units of royal soldiers dressed in heavy chain-link
armor. The cloudless days multiplied from a few to a
dozen to two dozen. Blue shadows moved across the
plains, and the mountains lazed like tawny lions on the
horizon. At night Pacorus fell from his camel, sore and
half-asleep.

Chapter 11

The caravan turned south from the green fields along the Caspian Sea and skirted the sandstorms at the western edge of the Dasht-e-Kavir Desert. A little more than a month after leaving Merv, the men and animals climbed into the Zagros Mountains. The late summer nights were chilly, and each morning Pacorus wiped light frost from his saddlebags.

One night the caravan stopped on a plain beneath a ring of somber cliffs. Pacorus hauled the saddle off his camel and set to the routine—rub down, feed, water, and tether his animal. He was tired and hungry and didn't hear the gallop of horses.

"Quick," Vardanes ordered. He pulled Pacorus behind him and took out his dagger. The ground

vibrated under the hooves of the circling riders. Some of the strangers carried torches. Others were dark forms that moved in and out of the light. The captain of the robber band pulled his chestnut stallion to a halt, and the other riders reined in their horses.

"What's going to happen?" Pacorus whispered. His heart thudded against his ribs.

"I'm not sure yet. Wait here while I find out." Vardanes stepped toward the caravan leader.

Pacorus reached into his saddlebag and found Susam's pouch. He pushed up his roomy, leather vest and stuffed the blue silk under his shirt. Then he tucked in his shirt and smoothed down the soft leather. The silk lay flat against his chest.

The robber captain dismounted and entered the circle of merchants. "Good evening, gentlemen," he said. "Welcome to our province. We always enjoy having visitors, and we're sure that you'll be generous guests. My men will walk among you. Empty all your gold and silver into our bags. Don't even think of holding back."

The caravan leader was silent. Then with a slight gesture, he motioned the thieves into the gathering. Pacorus gasped. The merchants, even his own father, had given in. Some of the robbers dismounted and drew their knives. They spread out among the merchants. Vardanes made his way back to Pacorus.

"Hand it over." A robber held out a filthy bag. His sheepskin coat reeked of sweat. Pacorus stepped back,

but Vardanes took out his money pouch. He poured his gold and silver coins into the robber's bag and then turned his own pouch inside out.

"I like a merchant who's honest," the robber said. His mouth opened on flat, toothless gums, and he howled at his own joke.

"Yes, my father's honest." Pacorus couldn't hold back. He took one step forward, then another. "He works hard, and he's fair, and you've no right. You're scum, you're..." An explosion hit Pacorus between his shoulder blades.

His body rushed forward, and his forehead slammed against the ground. He tasted dirt and heard the thief laugh. "That's right, merchant. Teach your son respect, and he'll care for you in your old age."

The splintering sensation in Pacorus's back and chest eased. He held his breath and sat up. "Foolish boy." Vardanes pulled him to his feet with a viselike grip. "Silly, ignorant child. You could have killed us all. I thought you had more sense."

Pacorus didn't know what to say. He was hot, then cold. He shivered. His teeth chattered. Vardanes took off his cloak and draped it over his son.

The entire scene had changed. The outlaws had remounted, and their horses stamped and tossed their heads. The robber captain gave a sign, and his men threw down their torches. With bloodcurdling screams, they galloped off into the darkness. Pacorus drew the

folds of the cloak tight and felt Susam's pouch.

He crossed his arms over his chest. The blue silk was warm and safe. He turned to tell his father he was sorry, but the signal to load the caravan drowned out his words. His father moved away. Pacorus leaned down and picked up his saddle.

The morning star appeared in the blue-black sky. Single file the men and camels moved through the pass. All eyes strained ahead to see the plain leading to the Tigris River.

Chapter 12

Two days after the robbery, the caravan reached the floodplain of the Tigris and Euphrates Rivers. The merchants had no money, so they sold some trade goods to buy fresh supplies. Pacorus waited, but his father never mentioned the robbery. Instead, to pass the time, Vardanes taught Pacorus phrases in Greek and explained the history of the region.

"The land between the Tigris and Euphrates Rivers," he said, "is the center of Parthian civilization. The ruler Hammurabi wrote famous law codes on huge stone tablets in his city of Babylon. Later the Chaldean king, Nebuchadrezzar, built water systems and terraced gardens. The Persian kings linked the ends of their empire with royal roads. Alexander the Great brought us

Greek culture and language. Our people have created one of the finest civilizations in the world."

Pacorus was proud. His ancestors had overcome many hardships. His father and the merchants would be successful, despite the robbery. If only Pacorus could find a way to make up for his own foolishness.

The caravan crossed the Tigris River on a floating bridge. The heavy wooden rafts, loosely lashed together, shifted and dipped as the camels walked across. From the Tigris, the caravan followed the path through the fields to the Euphrates. Golden wheat blazed under a milky blue sky. The caravan made camp on the banks of the Euphrates, and a handful of men appeared with tall, stout rods. They offered to pole the caravan across the river on separate rafts.

When his turn came, Pacorus sat on the edge of the thick, damp logs and let his feet trail in the water. Along the riverbank, a group of women washed clothes. Some children waded into the water, kicked, and sprayed the air. An older boy taught a little girl to swim.

Susam, his mother, his friends, the little garden in Merv all seemed very far away. Pacorus wondered why he'd left. What was the point of selling the blue silk in Palmyra? The night in the Zagros Mountains had only shown his father that he still acted before he thought. He might always be that way. But at least he could apologize. In a few days, when they were closer to

Palmyra, he would talk to his father.

Beyond the Euphrates, the caravan entered the Syrian Desert, the last leg of the journey. The air was hot and dry. Herds of wild antelope, gazelle, and ostrich moved across the plain. Golden-throated game birds flew up from the sweet-scented scrub. Pacorus broke away from the caravan to chase hares and foxes. At night the wolves howled beyond the campfire. One evening he put down his plate and turned to his father.

"I've been thinking about the robbery, Father," he said softly. Vardanes didn't answer but tore a last piece of bread in half. Pacorus forced himself to go on. "I think about the robbery all the time. And I'm sorry. I really am. I'm sorry I didn't think."

Vardanes was silent. The crease formed between his brows. Pacorus thought of the stillness before thunder.

"You're right," Vardanes said. "You didn't think. That's the way you are. At home you argue. You run in and out. You never really listen. And I'm partly responsible. I haven't done enough to check you. A good trader knows when to take risks and when to hold back."

"I'll be more careful now," Pacorus said. He met his father's eyes.

"Good." Vardanes smiled, and his frown smoothed out until only a faint line remained.

Pacorus vowed he would hold himself in check. He would sell his blue silk in Palmyra, but he wouldn't

take the first offer. He would wait and make counter offers until he had the price he wanted. His father would see.

Two months after leaving Merv, Pacorus and Vardanes unloaded their camels at the huge caravansary at Palmyra. Animal dealers milled about selling fresh camels and buying sick animals for leather and meat. Every trader and driver seemed to speak Persian, Greek, and Aramaic.

"Watch our animals and goods," Vardanes said to his drivers. "We're going to the bazaar to find our kinsman Tiridates." Pacorus checked on the blue silk one last time. It was safe inside his own saddlebag. Vardanes searched his silks for a present.

"Take this one." Pacorus picked out a scarlet bolt embroidered with golden clouds and flowers. It would tell his relatives that his father was an important merchant.

"You have a good eye, my son," Vardanes said. Pacorus was surprised and pleased. Here was something he could do well. With the red silk tucked under his arm, he set off beside his father.

Chapter 13

Pacorus jumped quickly out of the way. A cart piled high with unfamiliar fruits rumbled past. He followed Vardanes down a narrow side street, missed a turn, and found a mountain of salted fish blocking his way. He retraced his steps. His father had disappeared. There was no sign of him. Pacorus started in one direction, then stopped. He was lost. Vardanes emerged from a shop just ahead of Pacorus and said, "Come and meet Tiridates."

A small, round man with lively green eyes and a full beard ran from behind the counter. He hugged both father and son. "These are my relatives from Merv," Tiridates said to his workers. "How was the journey? Did you have trouble coming through the mountains?

Wait. Don't tell me now. Join our family for dinner."
Tiridates hustled his visitors out the door and smoothly
navigated them through the crowded marketplace, all
the while explaining his business to Pacorus.

"I organize caravans for wealthy merchants. Just a
word and the animals, the supplies, and even the
weapons are ready. I recommend guides, camel mas-
ters, and caravan leaders. There's no one I don't know
in Palmyra."

"But everyone here speaks a different language,"
Pacorus said.

"Only three or four," Tiridates corrected. "I speak
Greek, Aramaic, and Persian. I deal with the king's
officials in Greek, but I keep my accounts in Aramaic.
With my family and friends, I use Persian." Pacorus
looked impressed, but Tiridates hastened on. "Of
course, to be really successful I have to understand
other people's customs as well as their languages.
And I have to have common sense. A fool with five
languages can still go out of business."

Pacorus remembered his father's comment that reck-
less was not the same as brave. Would he catch himself before he made another mistake?

Several hours later, Vardanes and Pacorus sat with
Tiridates and his family at the evening meal. The servants had set soft rugs and low tables on the roof of
the flat-topped stone house. The evening breeze bent
the flames of small oil lamps. The adults sat at one

table, speaking in relaxed tones. Pacorus joined his three cousins at another. Between courses the twins played with the wooden horses Pacorus had brought them. They galloped them between the plates and made them rear and fight. Tongue-tied, Pacorus sat beside his pretty cousin, Dinna, and mumbled one word answers to her questions. He was grateful when a servant offered him clusters of purple grapes from a serving platter.

After pulling off some of the fruit, Pacorus stared at the platter. He could see right through it. What kind of material was this?

"The plate is made of glass," Dinna said, as if she could read his thoughts. Her light voice floated above the adults' hearty laughter. "You've never seen glass? It's made in Egypt, a country along the Mediterranean Sea, west and south of here."

"But what is it? Some kind of clay that lets the light shine through?"

"You'll laugh when I'll tell you," Dinna said. "The plate is made of sand." Pacorus smiled. "See. I said you'd laugh. A caravan leader once told me that the glassworkers heat the sand so hot that it melts and turns clear. Then they mold it into the shape they want and let it harden."

Pacorus took some more grapes and passed the platter. By the end of the meal, he could barely hold his eyes open. His head nodded forward. Vardanes

noticed, offered his thanks to his hosts, and promised to return for another meal.

Chapter 14

Over the next few weeks, Vardanes sold his goods during the day and dined with Tiridates each evening. Pacorus followed his father from one merchant to another and gradually learned his way around the marketplace. When Vardanes sent him on small errands, the boy began to use the Greek words that Dinna taught him each evening.

Vardanes took his silks to Zebida, son of Maliku. Zebida was honest but shrewd. After two weeks of bargaining, all the elaborate silks had been sold. Vardanes had only two bolts of pure white, and Pacorus had his blue silk.

The morning of the sale, Pacorus carried Susam's woolen pouch and walked in silence with his father.

Pacorus hardly noticed the carts or the vendors' shouts. His palms were sweaty, and his mind raced. His opening figure would be high, but his bottom price was fair. He could come down a little, but no argument or offer would make him take less than what the silk was worth. The sale would show his father what kind of trader he could be. Vardanes stopped at the door of Zebida's shop.

"Give me your blue silk," his father said.

Pacorus looked puzzled.

"Give it to me. I'll add it to my white bolts and get one price for the lot."

Pacorus tried to speak, but he couldn't. In his mind, he was inside the shop. His silk was spread on the thick rugs in the back room. He had started to bargain.

Sunlight hit his eyes. He squinted and saw his father was holding out his hand. Pacorus clutched the blue silk tighter.

"My son," Vardanes said, "do you really think that you can sell your silk by yourself? A boy of eleven dealing with a man as experienced as Zebida?"

Pacorus was silent, but his burning cheeks gave him away. Vardanes drew him into the shadow of a nearby arch. "I should have talked to you before. It's your silk, so, of course, you expect to sell it. But that's not the way you'll become a trader. You must watch and learn from older men. Give it to me. I'll sell it for you."

Nothing could be done. Pacorus handed over the silk, and Vardanes entered Zebida's shop. Pacorus stepped in behind him.

In the back room, the two men settled opposite one another, and Pacorus sat to one side between them. Zebida examined the two bolts of white and the rippling folds of the pale blue silk. Pacorus couldn't read the shop owner's expression. "I'll take these silks as one lot," Zebida finally said and offered a reasonable price. Pacorus held his breath.

"They are worth much more," Vardanes said. "They'll sell for a nice profit when you take them to Damascus."

Zebida stroked his beard. "They are, indeed, excellent fabrics. The Romans are very anxious for silk, but they are also a changeable people. One can never keep up with their ideas about fashion."

The conversation drifted to a halt. Pacorus looked from one man to the other. Vardanes spoke again, "These fabrics are very valuable. You can see yourself the quality of the weaving." Another silence. Vardanes made a suggestion. "Why not pay one sum for the white silks and another for the blue?"

Zebida considered. Then he made a better offer for the whites and a very good one for the blue. A trace of satisfaction passed over Vardanes's face. "I accept your offer for the white silks, but I'm not satisfied yet for the blue. It's a rare piece. The Chinese trader who

sold it to me valued it greatly."

Zebida lowered his eyes and folded his hands. "My last offer stands."

Pacorus compared Zebida's figure to his own top price. It was very close. He turned to smile at his father, but Vardanes was reaching for the blue silk. He was folding it up and shaking his head. He had rejected Zebida's offer.

It wasn't fair! Pacorus wanted to grab his father's hands. He wanted to tell him to stop, but he choked back his words. He tasted dirt and heard the robber laugh. His outburst in the Zagros Mountains rushed through him and kept him silent. He could only watch as the silk became smaller and smaller. Now it was the familiar square ready to slide back into Susam's pouch.

"I double my offer for the blue," Zebida said.

Pacorus jerked around.

"Double," Zebida repeated. The new figure washed over Pacorus and then took hold. The amount was high. Very high. Higher than he'd ever expected. He looked at his father. Vardanes drew his brows together and glanced at his son. Pacorus recognized the question and gave a single nod.

"I accept your offer," Vardanes said. "You're a man of excellent judgment." Zebida handed the silks to a servant and paid Vardanes with gold.

Pacorus wanted to jump up. His silk was leaving, and he would never see it again. I've changed my

mind, he started to call out. He jammed his fist against his mouth. Now was the time to be brave and not foolish. The servant stacked the silk on a shelf. Pacorus looked away. Vardanes rose, and Pacorus followed him without a backward glance.

Outside the shop, Vardanes gave Pacorus the money from the sale of his silk. Together they strolled through the crowded lanes. At one stall, Pacorus picked up a glass goblet.

"You could buy glass," Vardanes said, "but it would probably break before you got home. Your investment would be wasted." Pacorus put his hand behind the goblet. He wriggled his fingers, and they looked like minnows in a clear stream. "Still," Vardanes continued, "if it were wrapped first in woolen blankets and then in rugs, it might arrive safely."

"Glass would bring a lot of money, wouldn't it?"

"Yes. Especially because you'd have the seller's advantage. Glass is so rare in Merv that many would want it. If one merchant didn't offer your price, another would. You, as the seller, would have the edge over the buyer."

"Like the blue silk!" In an instant, Pacorus understood.

"Yes," Vardanes said. "Like the blue silk. Zebida recognized that the silk was unusual, but he didn't know if I also understood it. When I put the silk away, I showed him that I had the seller's advantage. He gave in and paid the price we both knew the silk

was worth."

"I would have taken much less," Pacorus said.

"A typical beginner's mistake," Vardanes said bluntly. Pacorus looked up, but his father was smiling. "So Pacorus. Are you going to invest in glass?" Pacorus studied the goblets. Susam would like to see them.

"For now I think I'll buy just one, as a present." Pacorus lifted a tapered drinking glass with a pale green rim. He imagined sitting in the garden with Susam. He would ask her, "What has shape, holds water, and is the color of air?" Susam would think for a while and swing her feet back and forth. She would shake her head. She would say he was teasing her. He wouldn't answer or defend himself. Instead, he would bring out her embroidered bag and let her unwrap her present from Palmyra.

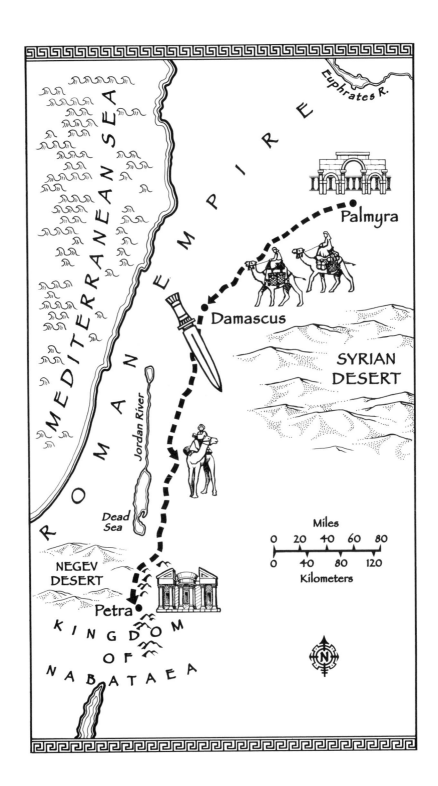

Euphrates R.

MEDITERRANEAN SEA

ROMAN EMPIRE

Palmyra

Damascus

SYRIAN DESERT

Jordan River

Dead Sea

NEGEV DESERT

Petra

KINGDOM OF NABATAEA

Miles
0   20   40   60   80
0   40   80   120
Kilometers

N

The Blue Silk
Journeys from
Palmyra to Petra

Chapter 15

Deep in the study of glass goblets, Pacorus didn't notice an older man, a Nabataean caravan guide, pass near him. Rabel Dushara was not tall, but he held himself very straight. A white scar crossed one eyebrow, and his deep-set eyes scoured the marketplace. He, too, had traveled with his father.

For twelve years, from when Rabel Dushara was six to when he was eighteen, he'd ridden with his father at the head of caravans. Each night his father had quizzed him on the day's trails. After twenty years on his own, Rabel Dushara had the desert routes burned into his mind. The desert was in his heart as well. He was at ease only in its bleak hills and empty valleys.

Rabel Dushara turned down a crowded alley and

entered the shop of Zebida, son of Maliku. Angry
voices rose from the back room. He tried not to listen.
The door flew open, and a lean man wearing a red turban rushed out. "Camel driver or nothing, Aretas," a
deep voice called. "See the camel master by dawn tomorrow." But Aretas didn't stop or seem to hear.
Without looking, he shoved Rabel Dushara against the
wall and stormed out of the shop.

A servant ushered Rabel Dushara into the back room.
The man with the deep voice introduced himself as the
merchant, Matthias ben Johannan. Zebida offered
fresh figs and dates and then came to the point. "I'm
organizing an important caravan, two hundred merchants and five hundred animals. Matthias will be the
expedition leader. You've been recommended to us by
Tiridates, the caravan supplier."

Matthias picked up the discussion. "We've already
selected the trading spots. The caravan will go first to
the markets of Damascus in Roman Syria, then along
the trade route east of the Jordan River through Roman
Judea. After the last town, the caravan will head due
south down the desert valley to Petra."

Rabel Dushara was pleased with the route and the
destination. His aunt and uncle and their six lively
children lived in Petra, a caravan town in the kingdom
of Nabataea. They were his only family now, and he
was always eager to see them. "The journey from
Palmyra to Petra can take three or four or even five

weeks, depending on the number and length of the trading stops," he said.

"It's mid-autumn now," Rabel Dushara said, thinking out loud. "If we start in the next few days, we should arrive before the winter rains begin. After that the mountain trails will be too dangerous for a large caravan."

"Then you'd be interested?" Zebida asked.

"Perhaps," Rabel Dushara said. A bolt of blue silk on a shelf across the room caught his eye. It was the Nabataean color of good luck, the shade of turquoise mined in the desert near Petra. His aunt and uncle would like to see this cloth. His uncle might sell it in his stall. "I'll take two months wages and that bolt of blue silk."

Zebida looked at the silk. "The success of this caravan is very important to me. If the blue pleases you, it's yours."

On the morning of departure, Rabel Dushara arrived early at the caravansary. He had a large basket of clothes, a water bag, and a smaller basket with his wages and the blue silk. These had been packed for hours. Now he strapped them onto his camel. His animal was skittish, and he reached out to stroke its neck.

"Hold back your animal," a voice behind him called out. "Can't you see I'm loading up?" Rabel Dushara turned. The speaker was Aretas from Zebida's shop. He was wearing the same red turban.

"My camel's not in your way," Rabel Dushara said. "You've got plenty of room." His camel reared and strained at the tether.

Aretas thrust out his fist. "I've already told you. Keep your animal away from me!"

"My camel didn't bother you!"

"I've got eyes. I can see for myself."

"You're blind! Blind and crazy."

"You can't control your own camel. What fool let you into this caravan?"

"Zebida hired me as the guide," Rabel Dushara said. A shiver of fear ran down his back. Why wouldn't this man give up?

"Guide?" Aretas spat. "I should be the guide."

Rabel Dushara fit the pieces together. Aretas had been rejected as the caravan's guide. Now he was on the trip as just another camel driver, and he was angry.

"Too proud to have me as your guide?" Rabel Dushara asked. "Then stay here and clean up after the camels."

Aretas started to answer, but he stopped and peered at Rabel Dushara. His faced twisted. "I know you. It's the scar." He took a step closer. "Five years ago, you led the trip down the Euphrates to the gulf. Half the caravan, some of my friends, died from swamp fever. You killed them."

"No, I didn't. I tried to save them." Rabel Dushara kept his voice calm. A trumpet sounded. The caravan was ready to leave. He mounted and spurred his camel

to the head of the line. The trip to the gulf came back to him.

From the very start, the caravan had traveled through rain and heat. A dark cloud of mosquitoes had hovered over the men. Day after day, they'd smeared their bodies with grease and had shrouded themselves in stifling woolen cloaks. Still the insects had crawled into their clothes and had bitten their legs, necks, arms, lips, and eyes.

The men had burned with fever. Under their cloaks, their temperatures had soared until they collapsed over their animals. Each evening the sick men had laid on blankets, staring vacantly at those who brought them water. In the morning, Rabel Dushara had helped bury the dead. Weeks later the expedition, half of its original size, had straggled into the gulf towns.

Camel noises brought Rabel Dushara back to the present. The caravan was leaving Palmyra in chaos. The line moved out too slowly, and the camels brayed and stumbled. Rabel Dushara rode ahead to the desert road. He wanted to free himself from the tangle of riders, animals, and memories.

Chapter 16

For five days, the caravan to Petra wound its way over the faded lavender ridges and across the Syrian Desert. One evening the expedition stopped at a small oasis, and Rabel Dushara led his camel to the brackish water.

"Move your animal out of my way." Aretas stood beside him. He held a pot and clearly intended to scoop out water for washing.

"The animals drink first," Rabel Dushara said. "Then we'll get water for ourselves."

"You should grovel and beg for water," Aretas said. His mouth twisted, and he flung down his pot. It clanged against a rock and rolled to the side. Rabel Dushara quickly calculated his odds in a fight. He weighed more, but Aretas was taller and angrier.

A small group of drivers glanced over. "What's the problem, Aretas?" one of them asked. Aretas didn't answer. He crouched low in the sand, brought his hands up, and angled out his elbows. The men moved back.

Aretas howled and charged. Rabel Dushara ducked, pivoted, and pounded Aretas on his shoulders. The camel driver grabbed the guide's arm and twisted it behind his back. Rabel Dushara bent low and flipped the younger man onto the ground.

The two rolled in the sand and mud. Aretas, quicker and stronger, reached for the guide's neck. Rabel Dushara spread his fingers and aimed at his attacker's wild eyes.

Aretas knocked the guide's arm back over his head. Rabel Dushara touched something soft and smooth in the sand. He grabbed the loose red turban and flung it full force. Aretas gave a shriek and clawed at the sand in his eyes.

Rabel Dushara scrambled to his feet. Aretas followed, ready to swing again. Matthias appeared out of the evening shadows.

"Hold him," he said. His deep voice brought the onlookers into action, and two of them seized Aretas. Rabel Dushara stood to one side, panting, glad the fight had ended.

Matthias picked up the red cloth from the sand. "Aretas, you've been in fights since we left Palmyra.

Saddle your camel and leave."

Aretas jerked his arms away from the men who held him. He took his red turban from Matthias. "What about my wages? I was hired to go to Petra."

"Here's a week's pay." Matthias threw a handful of Roman coins on the sand. "Be grateful. It's more than you deserve."

"And you." Aretas turned to the semicircle of men. "Cowards, all of you." He pointed to Rabel Dushara. "There's your guide. He led the trip to the gulf. Half the caravan died along the way. Now he's taking you to the desert. And you'll follow. The vultures will pick out your eyes, but still you'll crawl after him."

A murmur passed through the crowd. "Get out," Matthias said as he moved toward Aretas. "If I see you again, I'll put you in chains and give you to the Romans in Damascus. They'll feed you to the lions."

With a cry, Aretas swept the coins from the sand. The crowd parted, and he disappeared toward the animals. A little later, Rabel Dushara heard the muffled gallop of a camel leaving camp.

In the morning, the caravan moved onto the paved Roman road. Damascus was a day away. Rabel Dushara dreaded his arrival. The city was so noisy he could never hear or think clearly. The walls and buildings blocked his vision. People jostled him, and he was always short of breath. He wanted to avoid Damascus and move south into the familiar landscape of the desert.

Chapter 17

"Give up your idols!" a preacher in a brown tunic stepped in front of Rabel Dushara. "Accept the true God. He will forgive your sins." The man pinned Rabel Dushara with an unblinking gaze. The crowd in the Damascus square pressed around them.

"Every day, every hour, death approaches." The preacher's hot breath pushed his words closer. "No one escapes." He raised a finger beside his eye. "Repent, sinner, and the God of mercy will grant you everlasting life."

Rabel Dushara turned and shouldered his way out of the crowd. The man whirled around. At the top of his voice, he chanted and called out. More people gathered. Some jeered, and others prayed. Without

warning three Roman soldiers pushed their way through
the crowd. They grabbed the preacher and hurried him
down a side street. The crowd shouted in protest.

"Well, what did he expect?" A heavyset woman
peered out from her stall.

"Who was he?" Rabel Dushara asked.

"He says he follows a prophet named Jesus, the
Messiah." The woman drew her black shawl around
her. "He preaches that his god actually loves him. I
don't believe him, and the Romans consider him a
troublemaker. Of course that only means more business for me." The counter of the woman's stall was
piled high with swords and daggers. "Here," she said.
"Try this one."

Rabel Dushara took the knife. The bronze handle,
engraved with swirling designs, fit his grasp in a reas-
suring way. He tapped the steel blade against his palm
and ran his finger lightly over the razor-sharp edge.
He had an old knife in his pack. He didn't need a
new one. Still he savored the balance between the
blade and the handle.

"You look like someone who knows the value of a
fine weapon," the woman said. She ran her eyes up
his face to the scar across his eyebrow.

Yes, he could take care of himself. But what had the
preacher said? Death comes closer. No one escapes.
Perhaps it wouldn't hurt to have a special knife. "I'll
take it," Rabel Dushara said and put his coins into the

shopkeeper's plump hand.

"You won't be sorry." The woman handed him a soft, leather sheath.

Rabel Dushara headed for the caravansary. The new dagger comforted him. He was glad to have it.

That night he slept fitfully. The tread of a guard woke him. A little later, a camel brayed, and a driver spoke quietly. In the middle of the night, his door opened.

A tall shadow slid through and pressed itself against the wall. Metal gleamed in the moonlight. The figure inched along the rough plaster toward the baskets. Rabel Dushara waited until the thief bent to pick up the smaller basket. His new knife lay ready beside him.

"Death to you, son of a scorpion," he yelled as he sprang up and hurled his dagger. It flew across the room.

"Ayyyy!" A cry erupted from the dark. The knife clattered to the floor, and the thief fled.

"Guard! Catch him!" Rabel Dushara dashed into the courtyard, but in the confusion, the thief slipped away. Rabel Dushara shook his fist at the air and cursed, "May the great Tyche, goddess of fortune, lure you to the heart of the desert and leave you forever."

Back in his room, Rabel Dushara lit a shallow oil lamp. He opened the smaller basket and lifted out a heavy sack of gold. The blue silk glimmered up at him. He breathed a sigh of relief.

A guard appeared at the open door. "We caught this man running out the gate," he said. "Is he your thief?" Rabel Dushara raised his oil lamp until it shone on a torn white shirt and the unraveled end of a red turban.

"Aretas," he said. "He's a worthless camel driver. He started out with us from Palmyra, but our caravan leader threw him out for fighting. He must have ridden ahead to Damascus. He would have killed me."

"I came for my full wages," Aretas said. "I should've been paid for the whole trip. I should've been the guide. You've tricked me twice out of what's mine." He moved his hands, and the chains of his wrist cuffs clanked. Almost gently he said, "You think the gods are on your side. But I know better. No one's luck holds forever. When the gods are ready, your turn will come."

"He admits it," Rabel Dushara said. "He was going to rob and murder me." His voice was loud, but hollow. "Take him to the Romans."

The guard drew Aretas away, and Rabel Dushara picked up his knife. He cleaned it and put it back in its sheath. He lay down again, but sleep was impossible. He waited for morning.

Chapter 18

The oasis ahead is dry," Rabel Dushara said. He pulled his camel to a halt beside Matthias.

"This is the second day without water." Matthias looked at the rough hills and the gritty red land around them. The caravan had left Damascus a week ago, had passed the last trading stop, and was now heading for Petra.

Each evening Rabel Dushara had led the men to a waterhole he had used for years. The first ones gave clear water, but those that followed were shallow, black pools fit only for the camels. Tonight's well was a sunken hollow under a ring of palms. The spare water bags were almost empty, the valley was an oven, and Petra was three days ahead.

"Maybe there's an oasis somewhere else," Matthias said. "One not far off our track."

Rabel Dushara had already asked himself the same question. He shook his head, and his message rippled down the line of merchants and drivers. Matthias gave the signal for the caravan to move on.

Rabel Dushara rode ahead. He no longer expected to find water. Instead, he tried to distract himself. He recalled cool winter wells and shaded rooms. He thought of all the other times he had traveled this same route. Sometimes a single waterhole would be dry, but never three, four in a row. It must be the heat, the drought. Herders near the Jordan River had told him that the spring rains had come early and been light.

Throughout the night and into the next day, the caravan pressed on across the desert. The sun barely seemed to move from its fiery position. Rabel Dushara looked up, and the red heat jumped out, as if waiting for him. He dropped his gaze, and a red turban lay on the sand. He blinked, and it was gone. No one's luck lasts forever, Aretas had said. When the gods are ready, you'll die in the desert.

The gods were ready. He closed his eyes. The grainy orange sunlight pressed against his eyelids, and his body swayed. He covered his eyes and imagined the soft, silky darkness of night. The stars flickered. He walked into a desert oasis and saw a tent under the palms. It was made of blue silk. He would rest inside.

He stepped closer, but the tent vanished. He opened his eyes. A range of low blue mountains rose ahead of him.

A small oasis was tucked behind the ridge of hills ahead. He had camped there once as a boy. In the evening, his father had draped a length of linen over a triangle of branches and anchored the cloth to the sand with small stones. The boy had curled up in the tent, sheltered and snug.

Rabel Dushara wheeled around his camel and headed back to the caravan.

"I know an oasis to the east," he said to Matthias. "It probably still has water, but it's a day out of our way."

Matthias looked at him. "Are you sure?"

"Yes," Rabel Dushara said. "I say we go to the mountains."

"To the east," Matthias called to the line of men behind him. Slowly the caravan changed direction. The mountains ahead now looked gray and parched. If the oasis had water, the hills gave no hint.

Rabel Dushara fought back new doubts. The mountain streams would be dry. The oasis was actually more to the north or two days to the east. The terrain seemed less and less familiar. He had never crossed the hills at this point, and he saw no landmarks. He had taken the caravan off the main route and sealed his own fate. His camel started up the mountainside.

At the top of the ridge, Rabel Dushara saw the first

of the dark-winged clouds. Too early. The rains weren't due for two more weeks. A moment later, the wind hit with an icy blast. Thunder boomed, and sheets of driving rain separated the men, shocking their heated bodies and blurring their vision.

"Watch out," Rabel Dushara warned the men behind him. His camel slipped, then recovered. The trail became slick, and other animals pulled away from the path. Camel drivers called to one another.

"It's too late!"

"The track is giving way!"

The rain turned the mountain into a mudslide. The camels stumbled, crashed into one another, and crumpled onto the path. The men struggled to stand up, but the mud sucked at their feet. Animals bellowed over the drivers' cries for help.

Matthias caught up with Rabel Dushara, "The animals are almost out of control. In a minute, they'll rampage down the hill, and some of the men will be trampled." Rabel Dushara looked at the trail. It boiled with brown water. His leather sandals had disappeared beneath the current, and the ground shifted under his soles.

His eye caught a narrow crease off to the side between broken shrubs and stunted trees. It was an accidental trail made by the small, wild donkeys that roamed the mountainsides.

"Turn the men this way," Rabel Dushara said and

pointed left. "I'll go ahead." He worked his way forward among the stones and bushes. At a bend, he looked back. The caravan was following.

Hours later at the oasis, while some of the drivers watered their animals and other men bound their bruises and washed off the mud, Rabel Dushara approached Matthias. "How bad are the losses?"

"Forty horses, twenty camels." Matthias said.

Rabel Dushara shuddered. "Once," he said, "half of my caravan died on an expedition to the gulf. The rest of us..."

"I've heard those stories," Matthias said. "Each trip is different. This time the wells were dry, but you found us another oasis. All the men are safe. I'm satisfied." Matthias turned to talk to the camel master. Rabel Dushara saw that the conversation and the incident were closed.

A day later, the rain stopped, and Rabel Dushara led the men south through the mountain passes. Around a bend, hundreds of tombs and even whole temples rose out of the rocks. This was his signpost. Petra was straight ahead.

Later that night, Rabel Dushara unpacked his gifts at the house of his aunt and uncle, an elderly man whom everyone called the "Old Nabataean." He had already told his relatives about Aretas, the drought in the desert, and the surprise autumn storm. He unwrapped the blue silk and held it out.

"This color is very unusual," the Old Nabataean said. "It reminds me of the turquoise we have here in Petra."

"Your silk is the color of good luck," his aunt said. Rabel Dushara smiled. She had always been a superstitious woman. Whenever he left Petra, she urged him to take special charms to protect himself.

"Perhaps it was good luck," Rabel Dushara said. His mind flashed back to the moment he had imagined the tent of blue silk. He had opened his eyes, the gray mountains appeared blue, and he remembered the oasis. He didn't want to think about the journey. For now he was happy to be with his family.

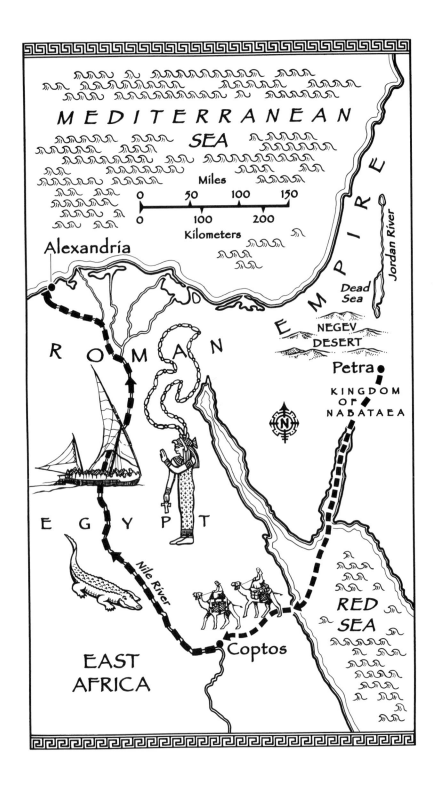

MEDITERRANEAN SEA

Miles
0   50   100   150

Kilometers
0   100   200

Alexandria

Jordan River

Dead Sea

R O M A N

NEGEV DESERT

E M P I R E

Petra

KINGDOM OF NABATAEA

N

E G Y P T

Nile River

EAST AFRICA

Coptos

RED SEA

The Blue Silk
Makes Its Way
from
Petra to Alexandria

Chapter 19

"Make way! Move to the side! Citizen of Rome coming through." A tall slave waved his arms and shouted to clear a space. Behind him four men carried a traveling chair into the market. They lowered it to the ground, and a large man stepped out. He smoothed his tunic, tossed his spotless white toga over his shoulder, and surveyed the bazaar at Petra as if he owned it.

"Who's that Roman trader?" the Old Nabataean asked of the young Egyptian beside him. Firmus Octavius Parro traveled the long, thin triangle from his home base in Alexandria, Egypt, south to the port cities along the Red Sea coast of East Africa, and then north to Petra. Firmus looked up from his study of the

baskets of black peppercorns.

"He's Claudius Rufus Gallus. My grandfather and I met him years ago at the Red Sea ports." Firmus watched Claudius, and his jaw set like a runner before a race. "That was when we traded in gold and gems. Claudius Rufus was already wealthy, but he knew nothing about the markets south of Egypt. We helped him, and within five years all our merchants left us to deal with him."

"He didn't steal everyone," the older man said.

"No. You're still loyal, and you still have the finest turquoise and spices in Petra," Firmus said. The Old Nabataean had once been one of his grandfather's rivals, but over time they had become friends. Now, at twenty-five and in charge of his grandfather's spice business, Firmus considered the Old Nabataean a distant, elderly relative. His grandfather always asked for news of him and was happy when he heard that the Old Nabataean was well.

"Today I have something besides spices," the Old Nabataean said. He brought out a packet of linen and unfolded a bolt of pale blue silk.

Firmus studied the luminous folds. "I don't know anything about silk, but this piece looks very unusual. Where did you find it?"

The lines around the old man's amber eyes crinkled. "My nephew brought it from Palmyra two weeks ago. He says it gave him good luck on his trip."

"How much do you want?" Firmus asked. The Old Nabataean gave a figure, and a spark ignited inside Firmus. The price was steep, but he could pay it. One part of his mind argued that he should stick to spices, another part urged him to try something new.

"I'm interested," Firmus said. The Old Nabataean broke into a slow smile. In less than twenty minutes, Firmus owned the blue silk.

He was halfway across the market square with his new purchase, when Claudius Rufus Gallus greeted him. *"Salve,* Firmus Octavius."

"Salve, Claudius Rufus." Firmus slipped easily from Aramaic to Latin, the language of Rome.

"I'm surprised you're in Petra," Claudius said.

"I always come for the fall markets, but I only buy a few things." Firmus thought of Claudius as a huge sea monster who swallowed whole bazaars in a single gulp.

Claudius Rufus missed the insult and instead patted his money pouch. "When I travel, I trade. One never knows what a customer might fancy. Fickle tastes turn fine profits." He smiled at his clever phrase and looked around with a greedy glance. "This is my first trip to Petra. Know any interesting shops?"

Firmus leaned closer. "You might try the Old Nabataean." He tilted his head in the direction of the stall. "Everyone says that he gets special things from his nephew, the guide. I've never had any luck, but you might do better."

Claudius looked past Firmus to the small, weathered booth. "That hovel?" He raised an eyebrow. "Doesn't look like much. But I might stop and see what he has to offer."

"Too bad I won't see your treasures," Firmus said. "I leave for the coast this afternoon." With polite good-byes and empty promises to see one another in Alexandria, Firmus and Claudius separated.

Firmus set off for the caravansary, fuming to himself. He was a better merchant than Claudius. His skills were sharper, and he had a better eye for quality. His tongue was quicker, too. But Claudius always won because he traded in Italy. No market in Egypt could match the high prices paid in Rome. No wonder Claudius had the money to buy whatever he wanted. He could always sell it for a small fortune back home.

A woman carrying a basket on her head bumped into Firmus, and he dropped his new silk. He picked it up, dusted it off, and looked at it again. If he could sell this rare silk in Rome, it would bring a handsome profit. He'd even have enough to start to trade again in gold and gems. The silk would help him turn the tables on Claudius and restore his grandfather's business and reputation.

Chapter 20

A week later, Firmus and his men crossed the Red Sea and traveled west across the Egyptian desert toward the Nile River Valley. It was the last month of the year, and the weather was warm and pleasant. Firmus detoured around crews of workmen replacing sections of the caravan track with a paved road.

"Ibi! Saxa demittite!" a worker shouted. Stones rumbled off carts into the roadbeds.

"What did he say?" Another man cupped his ear and shouted above the roar of tumbling rocks. A fellow worker, white as a ghost from the limestone dust, raced up and waved his pick.

"Dump the cobblestones over there, not here! *Asinus! Caudex!"*

"Blockhead yourself! We've been waiting since dawn. Let the others wait as long. After we hammer in these stones, our section will be finished."

"But look what you've done!" The ghostly worker threw down his pick. "All around you is desert. You've built a little piece of road in the middle of nowhere. Sometimes I think all the rocks are in your head!"

Firmus didn't mind the confusion and inconvenience at all. On his next trip, he'd travel a smooth, permanent highway. He caught himself. His next trip would be across the Mediterranean to Rome. He'd never been to Rome, although he'd always said one day he would go.

Now he had a reason for the trip, but suddenly he was uneasy. He didn't know a single person in Rome. Alone, without any contacts, how could he find a reputable silk dealer? He couldn't sell the blue silk to the first dealer he met. Often the best merchants, like the Old Nabataean, were the hardest to find. The task might be more difficult than he thought.

At Coptos, a small river port on the Nile, Firmus and his men transferred his goods to a ship. His servants made a comfortable corner for him beside the crates, and he settled down for the three-week journey northward to Alexandria. The boat cast off and raised its single sail.

Firmus spent the first week watching the life along the Nile. Deer and wild boar came to drink at dusk.

Water fowl spread their wings and rose squawking out of the reeds. Crocodiles slid off sandbars and disappeared into the murky water.

One night, during the second week on the river, Firmus woke to an argument on the other side of his crates. Two men stood near the railing. In the moonlight, Firmus caught the glint of a gold earring on the smaller man and the tightly curled beard of his broad-chested opponent. "I saw you," the smaller man said. "You cheated."

"You're dreaming," said the bearded figure. "I won by skill. You're a bad loser." The bearded winner turned to leave, but the loser reached out and pulled him back.

The bigger man whipped around and with all his might punched the other in the stomach. The smaller man groaned and sagged against the rope railing. The attacker cast one quick look over his shoulder then pushed the small man over the rope into the Nile. At the splash of water and cry for help, two sailors appeared and dragged away the bearded gambler.

Firmus rushed to the side of the boat and peered at the figure bobbing in the dark river. The man gave an ear-piercing scream and thrashed the black water into foam.

"Crocodile," said a sailor who had come to look.

"Firmus glanced around the deck. "Get a rope," he ordered.

"It's the will of the gods." The sailor didn't move.

"If the gods will it, he'll die on deck." Firmus grabbed a coil of rope from the top of a nearby barrel and unwound several lengths. The boat moved farther and farther on, but Firmus sailed the rope out over the water. It fell within an arm's length of the drowning man. He flailed toward the frayed strands and caught hold.

"Haul him in," Firmus shouted. Several passengers took up the thick hemp cord and reeled it onto the deck. The man in the water was closer now. His eyes were wide, and he stretched out his hand. Firmus reached over, grasped the ice-cold fingers, and drew the sodden body over the railing.

The man's head fell back, and his eyes had a glassy look. His short, white tunic streamed with water. Just below the ragged garment, his remaining leg knocked against a mangled, bloody stump.

"The river gods have spoken," said the sailor. Firmus laid the unconscious man on the deck, and the passengers backed away. An old woman with a reed basket pushed through the crowd.

"Out of my way," she said.

"Go tend to your childbearing women, Grand-mother." The sailors blocked her path. "There's no help for him."

The old woman's gray hair escaped in tendrils from her white woolen shawl, and her thin arm clutched her

ancient basket of medicines. Around her neck, she wore a golden chain with a small exquisite pendant of Isis, the ancient Egyptian goddess of the sea, protector of widows and girls.

"Isis," said the old woman, "was the first healer. She restored the body of Osiris her husband, after he had been hacked into fourteen pieces by his evil brother, Set. Osiris was left to drift in his coffin on the Nile, but Isis found him and brought him back to life. Now let me heal this man who has been thrown into the Nile."

Without waiting for permission, she came forward, and the sailors let her pass. She knelt beside the almost lifeless man, rummaged in her basket, and drew out a long strip of cloth. She wrapped the linen tightly around the man's leg to stop the bleeding.

During the next week, Firmus watched as the old woman mixed salves and ointments from her small bags. She changed her patient's bandages and applied herbs to his wound. Gradually, the injured man recovered. He sat up to drink and eat. One morning two sailors made a stretcher from an extra sail and gently lifted the patient into the canvas trough. The boat docked at a little village. The sailors carried him down the gangplank and up to a cluster of waiting relatives.

Firmus wanted to thank the healer and even to ask about her medicines, but she had retreated into a corner. Each time he looked for her, she seemed to be

dozing. He turned his attention to the passing shore and waited for the pyramids. He never tired of seeing the tombs that held the embalmed remains of the Pharaohs, the ancient kings of Egypt.

Chapter 21

Within a day of docking at Alexandria, Firmus repacked his baskets. He needed conversation, so he went to find the healer. She was at the rail, gazing over the water.

"It's the fisherman," she said before he could speak. "You pulled the poor gambler out of the Nile."

"I'm Firmus Octavius Parro. You're the one who saved his life."

"I'm Tullia Galina."

"You're a very good healer," Firmus said. "Probably no one even thanked you."

"Did anyone thank you?" Tullia smiled when Firmus shrugged his shoulders. "I didn't think so. Besides, we did what we thought was right."

"I deal in spices," Firmus said. "I'd like to learn about your healing herbs. Would you show me?" The old woman nodded and led the way back to her bundles. She seated herself, opened her basket, and laid out a sample of each powder and leaf. Firmus asked how the herbs were combined into medicines, but she shook her head and smiled. "The exact mixtures are the healer's secret."

Two hours later, she finished her explanations and packed away the last salve. She studied Firmus. "A darkness moves across your face. Something is bothering you. Tell me."

Firmus flushed. "You're right. I bought a beautiful bolt of blue silk in Petra. It was very expensive, and I told myself that I would sell it in Rome. Now I'm not so sure. I don't know any cloth traders, and I've never been to Rome."

The old woman was silent. Did she think him as foolish as he now felt? "My daughter might be able to help you," Tullia began. "Her late husband's brother is a merchant in Rome."

"Would she give me his name?"

"Perhaps. Come see us. We live on the Mediterranean side of Alexandria, very near the city docks." The old woman gave Firmus directions to her daughter's house. Then she excused herself to rest.

Late the next afternoon, the ship docked at Alexandria, and Firmus saw Tullia inch her way down the

gangplank.   Once on the quay, she was lost in the crowds.   He called his servants and was soon absorbed in unloading his goods.

Night had come by the time he arrived home.   The oil lamps cast pools of light in his small brick warehouse.   He stacked the baskets of spices on the dry floor and placed the blue silk, in its protective linen wrapper, on a shelf by itself.   He locked the storeroom, walked quickly through the house, and entered a walled garden.

In the moonlight, he crossed to a figure bundled in shawls and seated on a wooden chair.   "Sir," he said.

The drowsing man raised his head and opened his eyes.   He leaned forward, and his chair creaked. "Firmus."   The quavery voice floated out into the night air.   He covered his grandson's hands with his own.

"The trip to Petra was very successful," Firmus said. "Greetings to you from the Old Nabataean."

The old man gave a sigh.   A nearby servant bent over to adjust his pillows.   Firmus drew up a chair.   In a minute, the old man had closed his eyes again.

Chapter 22

During the month that followed, Firmus put Rome and the blue silk out of his mind. The spice trade, he reminded himself, was his living. After he'd sold the spices from Petra, he'd look for a boat. Then he'd visit Tullia and her daughter to ask for the name of a silk trader.

At the end of January, he went down to the harbor. He walked the quays that lined the Mediterranean waterfront like a stranger in a new town. The wharves were louder and busier than the Nile docks. The seagoing freighters with their deep hulls and tall masts dwarfed the tidy riverboats he knew so well. Even the air was different, salty instead of sweet.

"Firmus Octavius!" Claudius Rufus called from the deck of a freighter. He came slowly down the

gangplank. "Ah, Firmus," he said. "Looking for a passage to Italy? I didn't think you traded in Rome."

"When necessary, I go to Rome." Firmus didn't think it was completely a lie.

"I can hardly wait to get back." Claudius rubbed his hands and flashed his heavy gold rings. "I've such good things to sell. In Petra I found a set of ivory-handled knives and a dozen ebony chairs. Your Old Nabataean had several fine turquoise stones. A basket of gold goblets turned up at a port along the Red Sea coast. I'm also taking the jeweled necklaces I bought here in Alexandria. And you?"

Firmus had only one thing to take to Rome, but he certainly wasn't going to tell Claudius. He changed the subject. "Do you have a ship for the crossing?"

"Yes, the *Bast.*" Claudius pointed to the freighter he'd just left. "She'll be carrying the year's first shipment of winter wheat to Italy, so she'll be protected by a convoy of Roman ships. No pirates, a mere ten days at sea to the port of Ostia, a quick ferry trip up the Tiber River, and then a safe arrival in Rome at the start of the trading season." Claudius looked down his craggy nose in false modesty.

"With luck my ship will be as safe as yours," Firmus said. And she'll sail much faster, he added to himself. After more talk about trade and the weather, the two men parted, and Firmus returned to his search. By nightfall he was thoroughly discouraged. Some boats

were too slow, others too expensive. He started home through the narrow, dark streets.

Ahead of him, a shadow darted into the road, turned for an instant, and stared at him with a pair of gleaming, yellow eyes. Firmus bowed his head in reverence to the sacred cat. Without a sound, the animal disappeared into a nearby alley. Firmus took a step forward, and a small, sharp object hit his shoulder. He turned, and another grazed his cheek. In the street behind him, two boys, half-hidden, hurled pebbles in his direction. Firmus ran back toward them.

"Stop. You'll hurt her." A small girl knelt in the street. She held out her hands, her fingers spread wide apart, to shield someone on the cobblestones. Firmus veered around the little girl. The boys fled down a side street, and he retraced his steps.

He hunched down beside the child. "Was she hit?" The little girl nodded. Firmus gently turned over the figure. On the cobblestones, wrapped in her white shawl, was Tullia Galina.

"Will she be all right?" the small girl asked. Firmus looked at her. She must be a granddaughter. Tullia said that she lived with her daughter near the port.

"I think so," Firmus said. He wasn't at all certain. Tullia's breath was steady but very light. "We should get both of you home." He lifted the old woman into his arms and followed the girl. She wound her way through the maze of streets until, at last, she turned

into an alley and opened a heavy door. Firmus stepped across the threshold and into utter blackness.

Blindly, he followed the tap of the child's sandals. The smell of smoke filled the corridor, and a dull roar grew louder. The darkness shattered, and Firmus stood before flames raging in a huge, open furnace.

"Bring my mother in here." A young woman, perhaps his age, perhaps a year or two older, appeared beside Firmus. She was straight and tall, almost his own height. Her black hair was swept back to reveal an oval face, deep brown eyes, and a slender nose. She wore a linen tunic that belted at the waist and fell to her ankles. A gold chain with a small pendant of Isis gleamed around her neck.

Firmus followed her into a sparsely furnished chamber and laid Tullia on the simple bed. The young woman carefully removed her mother's sandals and covered her with a soft wool blanket.

"Thank you for bringing her," she said. "My daughter will show you out now."

"Of course." Firmus was reluctant to go. "May I come tomorrow? To see how she is?"

The woman shook her head, no. "It won't be necessary. Thank you anyway." She moved toward the door. The conversation was over. A few minutes later, Firmus passed through the fiery courtyard and the unlit corridor. The heavy door swung closed behind him, and he was out in the street.

Chapter 23

The next day, on his way to the harbor, Firmus stopped in Tullia's neighborhood. The streets were filled with peddlers, shoppers, and children. The boy pulling the cart of papyrus to the papermaker could have been one of the stone throwers from the night before. He brushed by Firmus without a sign of recognition. Firmus knocked on the heavy door. No one answered, so he opened it and walked down the corridor. He pushed open a second door. A burst of sunlight startled him, and he was back in the courtyard.

The fire still blazed, but now a half-dozen men, their faces streaked with soot, stood before the furnace and dipped long metal rods into the flames. Other men, on nearby benches, blew into their rods until

transparent bubbles bloomed at the far ends. This was a glassmakers' shop.

Tullia's granddaughter walked between the men, sweeping up the broken green and blue shards. She noticed Firmus and put away her broom.

He watched her neat, confident movements. She looked small, perhaps nine or even ten years old. In many ways, she resembled her mother. Her wide, brown eyes were the same, and she wore her dark hair as women did, drawn back and pinned up. It gave her a serious quality.

"I came to see your grandmother," Firmus said. "I hope she's better."

"Yes, much better." The child's face broke into a bright smile. Without hesitation she reached out, took Firmus's hand, and led him to her grandmother's room.

"Antonia?" the old woman called out from the bed. The room was shuttered and smelled of rosemary. "Antonia, is that you?"

"Yes, Grandmother. And I've brought the man who helped us last night." Antonia drew Firmus closer to the bed and opened one of the shutters. Light filtered into the room. Tullia struggled to rise. Antonia leaned into the bed, pulled the pillows up, and wrapped the white shawl around her grandmother.

Tullia was weak but alert and curious. "The fisherman," she said. She started to laugh but then winced and closed her eyes for an instant. "Antonia, here's the

fisherman I told you about, the one who rescued the gambler from the Nile. Now he's fished me out of the street. Bring him a chair. Fetch him a cool drink, too."

Antonia scurried about, and soon Firmus sat near the bed, while Tullia Galina explained what had happened. They had been coming home from a visit to a new mother when the boys saw them and had begun throwing rocks.

"They don't know any better," Tullia said. "Their parents tell them that I'm a healer, but they still think that I cast evil spells. Thank you for chasing them away and bringing us both home. How did you happen to be in our neighborhood?"

Firmus described his life with his grandfather and his unsuccessful search for a ship. Antonia, playing idly with the fringes of Tullia's shawl, stopped and looked up. "What about the *Isis?*" she asked her grandmother. "We're sending our glass to Rome on her. If we told the captain that Firmus was our friend, he'd make room for him."

"Perhaps so. Tell Firmus where to find the ship while I rest." Firmus stood up to leave, and Tullia invited him to come again.

In the courtyard, Antonia spoke to one of the glassblowers. Then she came running back. "I'm ready. Let's go."

"What about your mother?" Firmus said.

"She's at the warehouse packing the crates. She

won't mind. I run errands to the port all the time."
Antonia took a shawl from a hook on the wall, opened
the door to the stone corridor, and waited for Firmus.
Together they walked out into the street.

What ship, Firmus wondered, would Antonia know
that he had not already tried? At the end of the last
quay, she stopped before a small freighter. Streamers
hung from the stern while at the bow a wooden head
of Isis, goddess of the sea, jutted over the prow.

Antonia skipped up the gangplank, greeted the
sailors working on deck, and began to poke around the
cargo and equipment. She looked into open crates,
pulled the ropes that raised the piles of folded sails,
and climbed on the heavy stone anchors. "Antonia," a
big man with a booming voice called from across the
deck. "Did Lydia send you?"

"No, she's at the warehouse, packing glass," the girl
answered.

Firmus stepped forward. "Antonia brought me. I'm
looking for a safe and quick passage to Rome."

"Safe and quick. That's what you'll get here." The
strong, brown captain beamed around at his boat.
Firmus could easily believe him, the ship seemed so
sleek and trim.

"How long will the trip take?" Firmus held his
breath. Could he get to Rome before Claudius Rufus?

"My *Isis* is a fast ship," the captain said. "We'll
leave the third of March and arrive in six or seven

days. The drinking water is free, but you'll have to pay extra to use the ship's stove. Don't cut your hair or nails during the trip. You'll attract bad luck, and we'll throw you overboard."

Firmus agreed to all the rules, and, because he had no cargo, the captain lowered his fare. He paid the captain for his passage and turned to leave. Antonia stood at the gangplank. She pulled her eyelids down, and her eyeballs seemed to pop out of their pink sockets. Her thumbs tugged the corners of her mouth up into a horrid grin. She stared right at Firmus, and he struggled to keep a straight face. They were barely down the gangplank before they burst into laughter.

"Did you find the *Isis?*" Tullia was awake when Firmus and Antonia straggled in. They were tired, but happy. Antonia had shown Firmus all her favorite places, and now he knew his way around the harbor.

"Yes," Firmus said. "The boat's a beauty. It arrived last night, and I booked passage on her first run to Rome." The door to Tullia's room opened, and Lydia came in. Antonia ran up and wrapped her arms around her mother's waist.

"Lydia," Tullia said, "let me make introductions. This is Firmus Octavius Parro. He's not only the man who saved me from the boys last night, he's also the one who pulled the gambler from the Nile."

"Thank you again for your help," Lydia said with

reserved sincerity. "My mother is much better."

"When we were on the Nile," Tullia said, "I told Firmus that you might help him. He needs the name of a silk dealer in Rome."

Lydia was silent. She reached down and smoothed back a stray lock of Antonia's hair. "Sir, I appreciate your kindness to my family. Unfortunately, I can't help you."

"But, Mother," Antonia said, "Firmus already has a ship. I took him down to the *Isis,* and he's going to Rome on her."

Lydia pulled her hand from Antonia's head. "Who gave you permission to take him to the *Isis?* That's the ship we use."

"I gave permission," Tullia said. "The *Isis* is a fine ship, and Firmus needs a passage to Rome."

The color rose on Lydia's cheeks. "Well, now he has a ship, and that's enough from us. We've repaid our debts." She turned and walked out.

Tullia sank back against her pillows, "Please don't judge my daughter too harshly. I would tell you the name of the silk dealer, but he's Lydia's relative not mine. Only she can help you."

"Of course," Firmus agreed. "I think I should go."

Neither Antonia nor Tullia tried to stop him. Firmus walked out of the courtyard, troubled that he had upset everyone and disappointed that he still didn't have the name of a silk dealer in Rome.

Chapter 24

February passed while Firmus asked at the bazaar, along the waterfront, even at the Nile docks, but no one could give him the name of a reputable silk merchant in Rome. Now it was the first of March, and the *Isis* would leave in two days. He decided to return to Lydia's house and show her the blue silk. Perhaps if she saw it, she'd change her mind.

Toward evening, when he knew work in the glass shop tapered off, he took the blue silk in its linen wrapper and set off for Lydia's house. In the courtyard, the glassblowers had already stored their rods in racks against the wall and had left for the day. Antonia was sweeping the area around the furnace. She saw him, dropped her broom, and came running over.

"Grandmother and I have been so worried. We haven't seen you, and the captain of the *Isis* hasn't heard from you. You're still going, aren't you?"

Firmus held back his doubts. "Let's go visit Tullia. I'd like to see her." He moved toward the little room off the courtyard. Tullia might help him.

"Oh, no," Antonia said and motioned him away. "She's much better now. She's in the study with my mother. They're writing the loading lists to send with the glass. Come on." Antonia headed across the courtyard. Firmus hesitated. Would Lydia listen? What other choice did he have?

He caught up with Antonia, and they entered the house. In the study, the two women were seated at a large wooden table covered with rolls of papyrus. Tullia smiled as soon as Firmus entered. Lydia stood immediately. "Come in. I'm sure that Tullia and Antonia are delighted to see you."

She motioned for Firmus to take her chair. "I'll have a servant bring some refreshments." Firmus remained in the doorway.

"Please," he said. "Don't leave. I want to show you something." Lydia looked uncomfortable, but she sat down again and let Firmus draw up a nearby chair. Tullia cleared the table while Antonia came closer and leaned against her grandmother's shoulder.

The three women watched Firmus draw out the linen packet and unwrap the cloth. Lydia slid her hand

under the folds, and the blue silk sparkled like the waters of an iridescent lake. "Your silk is truly special," she said.

"My grandfather is a very old man, and his health is failing," Firmus began. "Once he was the finest gold and gem trader south of Egypt. Even though he did nothing wrong, he lost his business and his reputation. All my life, I've wanted to restore his honor. If I can sell this silk in Rome, I can start his business again. Will you help me?"

Lydia gathered herself and stood up. "I am a widow," she said. "Before my husband died, I promised to protect and carry on his trade. For three years, I've worked to improve the glassworks just as he had planned to do. Along the way, many have tried to hurt my business. That's the way it is. But I've been successful because I make the finest quality glass and because my clients know I'm honest.

"Your request seems so simple. You only want the name of a silk merchant." She raised her palms. It wasn't easy to explain. "If I write to my brother-in-law, he'll introduce you to an important silk dealer. This man, out of loyalty to us, will buy your silk for a fair price.

"Once you enter into our circle, my reputation will only be as good as yours. If you cheat and scheme, I am ruined. Can I trust you?" Lydia held very still. "No. I'm sorry. I can't. I won't take the chance."

Too disappointed to say anything, Firmus got up. He refolded the silk, wrapped it again in its plain linen cover, and placed it in the center of the table. He stepped to the doorway.

"Wait!" Lydia said, "your silk. You're forgetting your silk."

Firmus turned back to the little family. He knew he should resent Lydia's refusal, but instead he admired her determination. He'd never met such strong-willed women, and he wanted to honor them. "It's for you," he said to Lydia. "I was never supposed to take the silk to Rome. You were its destination all along. The silk belongs here."

Firmus walked out of the house into the courtyard. At the door to the corridor, he heard his name.

"Firmus," Lydia said, "Your silk." Her face was set, and she pulled on his arm.

Firmus studied the woman before him.

"Come back," Lydia said. "You gave us the blue silk out of respect. You won't hurt or betray us. I can trust you."

"Are you sure?"

"Yes. Completely."

Firmus stepped away from the door, and together they returned to the study.

Chapter 25

Two days later, the third of March, Firmus stood on the quay beside the *Isis* with his grandfather, Lydia, Tullia, and Antonia.

"Here. Take this with you," Tullia said, holding out a small packet of herbs. "They should help if you get sick at sea."

"Remember," Antonia squeezed his hand, "don't let bad luck get you." She crossed her eyes and stuck out her tongue.

Firmus grinned and gave her a quick hug. "Take care of your mother and grandmother."

"And we'll check on your grandfather," Tullia said.

"Do you have the silk?" Lydia asked.

"Yes, of course," Firmus said. The blue silk was

tucked in his bags beside the letter Lydia had written to her brother-in-law.

"Now go on, or you'll miss your boat." Lydia gave Firmus a little push. Firmus joined the other passengers. On deck he stepped around a group of musicians and athletes. A doctor settled two of his patients and explained for the last time that the sea voyage would cure their coughs. The captain gave the order to cast off.

Firmus found a spot at the rail. On the quay below, the crowd had boxed in a sedan chair. The four bearers looked familiar. They lowered the chair to the ground, and Claudius Rufus stepped out, his face beet red. He started to order the crowd out of his way.

"Claudius!" Firmus shouted, and the Roman looked up. His face deepened to purple as he recognized Firmus and realized that he was on his way. "Claudius," Firmus called out again. "Too bad we can't talk. My ship's about to sail. I'll look for you in Rome!"

Claudius turned back to his chair, barked a command, and climbed in. The chair swayed as it was lifted, and the bearers inched forward.

Firmus scanned the crowd. Antonia was swinging her arm above her head in long arcs of good-bye. Tullia had moved over to say a few words to his grandfather, and Lydia stood quietly, smiling up at the boat. The boat lurched, and Firmus grabbed the railing.

The ship was moving.

The port tugs, manned by powerful rowers, pulled the *Isis* away from the dock toward the lighthouse at the mouth of the harbor. The streamers at the ship's stern unfurled and snapped as they rode the breeze.

Firmus offered a short prayer to Isis, the goddess of healing, widows, young girls, and the sea. He prayed for a safe journey, successful trading, and blessings on the people he had left behind.

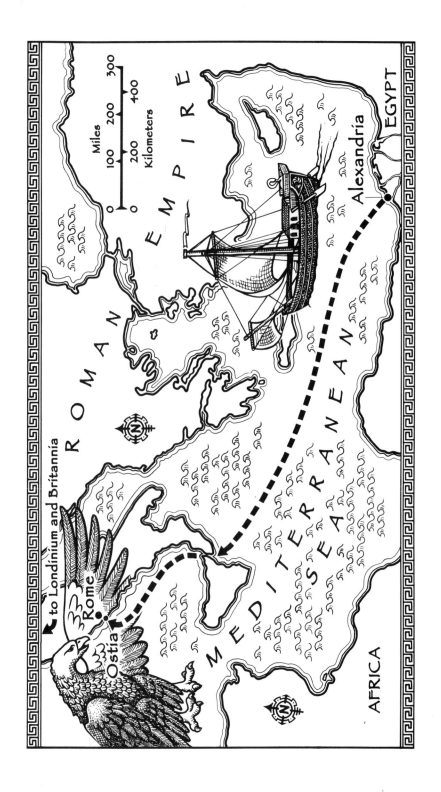

ROMAN EMPIRE

EGYPT

Alexandria

MEDITERRANEAN SEA

AFRICA

to Londinium and Britannia

Rome

Ostia

Miles
0   100   200   300

0   200   400
Kilometers

The Blue Silk
Arrives in Rome

Chapter 26

"All hail to Rome! All hail to the Eagle!" A standard-bearer held aloft a golden eagle. Its wings, poised for flight, glinted in the early morning sun. At the sound of a trumpet, the standard-bearer moved forward, and a regiment of imperial soldiers entered the broad square in the heart of Rome. On the edge of the cheering crowd, Julia Sabina and her slave, Melissa, watched the soldiers pass.

"How proud they are," Melissa said. "Are they from Britannia? Do they know Paulus?" Julia's childhood sweetheart, Paulus Valerius Scipio, had been in the Roman province of Britannia for the last year.

Julia studied the men's somber faces. "If they're from Britannia, they wouldn't know Paulus. He works

for the governor, not the generals." She stood lost in thought. Paulus was so far away, and she missed him so much. It was only March. He wouldn't be home until their wedding in June. Then they would return to Londinium together.

Sometimes she wished each day were only half as long. Other times she wanted the same day to last a week, so that she could put off leaving her family and friends. "Do I really want to go?" Julia asked aloud. Melissa stared at her mistress.

"But going to the market was your idea. You wanted to help Marcus pick out the fabrics for your wedding clothes. If anyone sees you, alone at the docks with thieves and butchers and traders, the rumors will fly. Paulus's father, the senator, might cancel the wedding. And I'm going to be in terrible trouble when your mother finds you've left the house. So if you've changed your mind, let's go home now."

Julia shook her head. "No. I'm not going home. If I don't go with Marcus, he'll choose fabrics to please my mother—all thick and plain and dull. My mother would wrap me in sheep fleece if it would guard the family's noble name."

"Well, don't just stand there," Melissa said. "Someone might recognize us." Julia pulled the hood of her cape over her wavy auburn hair, and the young women hurried on. A few minutes later, they arrived at the street of the tailors. Marcus was coming out of his shop.

"*Salvete,* Julia, Melissa," Marcus said without enthusiasm. "I was hoping you'd changed your mind."

"How often does Julia change her mind?" Melissa asked.

"Not very often." Marcus had known Julia since she was a little girl who insisted on approving each new ribbon that tied her simple tunics. She had grown up reflective, generous, and stubborn.

"I'll be fine with Marcus," Julia said. "Bring my mother here to meet us later this morning." Julia watched the dark-haired girl exchange worried looks with Marcus. "Go on. My mother won't eat you alive."

"But she'll definitely consider it," Melissa said. She waved good-bye and headed for home. The tailor, who was a head shorter than Julia and stoop-shouldered, set off with a rapid step. Julia hurried to keep pace.

They reached the wholesale market by the Tiber as the shops and stalls were opening. Burly workmen heaved tall oil jars with narrow, pointed ends from large wagons. Eager cooks crowded around spice stalls, ready to buy sauce for the evening meal. The merchants reopened their vats, and the tangy smell of fermenting fishheads filled the air. A distracted shepherd and his stubby-tailed dog herded a flock of goats to the butcher's stall.

"Get these goats out of here," shouted a workman. He stopped rolling his huge cask toward the wine merchant. A dozen small brown battering rams eagerly

attacked his barrel. The worker waved his arms and shouted curses, while the shepherd's little dog darted about, yelping and nipping to regather his goats.

Julia loved the confusion, and she hung back to watch the last of the goats brought back to the flock. When she arrived at the cloth merchant's booth, Marcus was already inspecting a variety of linens and wools. She fell to work, and in the end she agreed with Marcus on a range of colors and weights.

"Do you have anything special?" Julia asked. "I've had such a good time this morning. Surely you have something wonderful to make the morning perfect."

"Tell me what you have in mind," said the merchant, as he stroked his long chin and studied her.

"I want a beautiful silk. Something mysterious, like one of those transparent clouds that stretches across the sky at sunset." Julia extended her long slender arms so that the merchant could see her cloud.

"Julia," Marcus warned, "you know what your mother will say."

"I know. She'll say, 'Julia Sabina, you'll disgrace us the moment you step out the door.' But I don't care."

"I might have just the piece," the merchant said. He stepped to the back of his shop and returned with a thin package of rough linen. "I bought this silk yesterday from a new trader, a man from Alexandria. I paid him a small fortune, but the cloth's worth it."

The merchant shook out a cascade of pale blue silk.

For a moment, the beauty of the silk stilled all conversation. Julia touched the fabric. It shifted slightly and made the faintest rustle. "It's exquisite!"

"It'll be very expensive," Marcus said. He frowned, and his normally gloomy expression became even more dismal.

"But yesterday," Julia said, "my mother said to spare no expense."

"All right." Marcus yielded, and he added the silk to the pile of purchases. "We have to start back. Your mother will be waiting."

Chapter 27

W here did the blue silk come from?" Julia asked. She and Marcus were walking back to his shop with two heavily laden porters following close behind.

"The wholesalers tell me that silk comes from a country far to the east. The traders cross rivers too broad for any bridge and climb mountains so high that some of them die from lack of air. They travel over endless deserts and fight off thieves and outlaws. Finally, they come to the cities—Merv, Palmyra, Damascus, Petra, Alexandria."

"Are the cities as big as Rome?"

"I don't think so," Marcus said, "but I'd love to see them."

"What about Londinium? Would you visit me in

Britannia?"

"Should I come?"

"No," Julia said. "I guess not. I'm sure you won't find any silk. It will just be Paulus and me, some stuffy governor, and the Britons."

"Are you worried?" Marcus glanced over at Julia.

"Oh, Marcus," Julia couldn't hold back. "Sometimes I'm so scared. Britannia is so far away."

The conversation died, and the two walked on in silence. At Marcus's shop, his slave had already pulled back the shutters and had opened the door for business. Through the windows, Julia could see her mother examining some ribbons while Melissa waited nearby. Marcus and the porters took the purchases inside, and Melissa slipped out to greet Julia.

Julia handed over her cloak. "Was she very angry?"

Melissa opened her eyes wide and nodded. "Like Mount Vesuvius. One huge explosion after another." Julia gave Melissa a sympathetic look and then entered the shop.

"Julia!" Cornelia Lucilla swung around. Behind the layers of white makeup, red spots of anger burned on her cheeks and forehead. "If I had known, if I'd had even the slightest hint."

"I was very careful, Mother," Julia said. "Nothing happened to me. See? I'm fine."

"Think of your father, your future father-in-law! Suppose you had been seen with workers and sailors

 Between the Dragon and the Eagle *147*

and riffraff? Imagine what people would say!"

"But no one saw me." Julia's heart sank at the thought of a full-scale battle.

"Cornelia Lucilla." Marcus coughed lightly. "Let me show you the fabrics we bought. Julia was very helpful. She has your high standards."

Marcus unrolled the fabrics, and Cornelia turned to the counter. One after another, the bolts met her murmured approval, and her mood softened. At last Marcus unfolded the blue silk.

Before her mother could comment, Julia reached out and raised the fabric against her cheek. She moved to the silver mirror on the wall. For the first time, she saw that the blue of the silk matched the color of her eyes. "Look," she said, "it's perfect. It was made for me!"

"It probably costs too much," Cornelia said firmly. "Marcus can take it back."

"Oh. May I have it? Please," Julia pleaded.

Cornelia Lucilla extended her jeweled fingers toward the silk. Julia grasped her mother's hand. "All those other things—the things we argue about—what I wear, where I go, how I'll lose my reputation. They don't matter to me anymore. I'll change my ways. I'll do anything you want." Cornelia looked doubtful.

"Can't you see?" Julia rushed on. "The silk's a sign. It's a sign that I'll be happy, and that's all that really matters."

"The silk," Marcus said, his voice gruff and hesitant, "may well mean good fortune. For any silk to come to Rome from so far away is amazing. But this silk is different. I've never seen a piece so balanced in its weight and weave. And the color is simply magic."

Cornelia tried to look stern, but she quickly melted. "Very well, you may have the silk."

Julia threw her arms around her mother. Marcus checked some pins and thread. A moment later, Cornelia freed herself from her daughter's embrace, patted her reddened curls, and began to talk about dates for fittings.

Julia spread out the blue silk. Who had made it? How many hands had folded, wrapped, and carried it? How long had it traveled before it had arrived in Rome? She gathered it together, and a spark seemed to surge through her fingers and along her arm. With the lightest swirl, she swung the fabric over her head and let it drop around her shoulders. The silk settled over her back and arms, and she drew it around her. In its protective folds, she felt sure of herself. Now, she thought, I'm ready for my own journey.

Afterword

Despite many dangers, travel from China to Rome flourished at the turn of the first century A.D. This story of the blue silk, while fictional, is not unlike the journey of many real bolts of silk. In the end, however, not even the courage of traders and merchants could ensure the permanence of the Silk Road.

In A.D. 113, the Roman emperor Trajan became angry when he realized how much gold had left his empire for the coffers of Parthian merchants. To reclaim the lost revenue, he decided to invade Parthia. He would capture the kingdom, levy taxes on the sale of silk, and bring back some of the gold to Rome.

The Roman invasion had disastrous consequences. Fearing attacks on their caravans, Parthian merchants

refused to finance further expeditions. They cut back on their trade in silk and reduced the revenue that Trajan hoped to regain.

In addition, soldiers returning from the war in Parthia brought a terrible plague to Rome. Eventually, the plague covered all of western Europe. People died, incomes declined, and trade decreased. Fewer people could afford silk clothes.

In the east, at roughly the same time, China's stable relations with the nomads of the Western Regions began to break down. The Han dynasty itself grew weaker and finally split apart in A.D. 220. Without a peaceful western frontier or a strong imperial army to protect them, Chinese merchants refused to go to Parthia and instead refocused their trade on countries to the northeast and south. Those traders who ventured west chose the sea routes to India. Not until the voyage of the Italian explorer Marco Polo in 1271 did caravans again use an overland route.

Yet silk, with its luxurious feel and vibrant colors, never lost its allure for the Romans. In A.D. 552—four hundred years after the disastrous war in Parthia and under a secret order from the emperor Justinian I—two Christian monks made their way to India and stole a small number of silk moth eggs. Aware that they could be beheaded on the spot, the monks hid the eggs in their hollow walking canes and slowly made their way back to the emperor's court.

After they had returned to Constantinople, the capital of the Eastern Roman Empire, the monks carefully supervised the hatching of the eggs and the feeding of the moths until the cocoons of silk thread were formed. Soon a thriving silk industry existed, and the emperor could at last reap the rewards of having silk to sell in his own lands.

The Silk Road, with its successes and failures, introduced people to new goods and ideas, spurred technology, and stimulated travel. In the process of moving silk from China to Rome, ordinary people transcended the obstacles of geography, language, and culture to work together and to attain a common goal.